Medieval and Renaissance Series
Number 6

MEDIEVAL

AND

RENAISSANCE STUDIES

Proceedings of the Southeastern Institute
of Medieval and Renaissance Studies
Summer, 1974

Edited by Dale B. J. Randall

Duke University Press, Durham, N. C.

© 1976, Duke University Press

L.C.C. card no. 66-25361

I.S.B.N. 0-8223-0379-5

Printed in the United States of America

by Heritage Printers, Inc.

Foreword

There is a temptation—indecorous, doubtless, like most temptations—to begin these few comments with a passage from Wordsworth:

> Five years have past; five summers, with the length
> Of five long winters!

The fact is that when the Southeastern Institute of Medieval and Renaissance Studies opened its doors in the summer of 1974, five years had passed since its previous session. It was not for nothing, then, that the sign chosen to designate the 1974 session of the Institute was Corrozet's emblem of hope. And it is no mere empty verbal formula with which the Southeastern Institute expresses gratitude to the governing officials of the National Endowment for the Humanities.

Readers may better understand the whys and wherefores of the Southeastern Institute by glancing back at the introductory comments in earlier volumes of this series. Suffice it here to say that the original Institute was part of a cooperative program in the humanities established jointly with Ford Foundation aid by the University of North Carolina at Chapel Hill and by Duke University. It convened for five successive—and successful—years, during the summers of 1965 through 1969.

When the Institute flung wide its gates again in 1974, it had become national in scope. Whereas earlier sessions had drawn participants mainly from the Southeastern United States, the Institute of 1974 afforded an opportunity for concentrated, postdoctoral work to scholars and teachers from throughout the country. The primary aim of the Institute, however, remained constant: to enable teachers to work in their chosen fields at an advanced level with the dual end of attaining greater skill in teaching and enhancing scholarly productivity. Since heavy teaching loads are the common lot, and local library facilities are sometimes inadequate for specialized tilling in medieval and Renaissance terrain, the Institute has provided some of its Fellows with their first sustained opportunity since graduate school for intensive study. Moreover, it has also comprised a small, six-week community for the mutual acquaintance of far-flung scholars with similar or related interests.

Planning and work for the re-establishment of the Institute began in 1968. Members of the Institute committee, half from the faculty of the University of North Carolina at Chapel Hill and half from Duke University, convened sporadically but continually for several years. They explored a wide variety of funding devices, all the while waving credentials of past success, only to learn again and again the turn-of-the-decade definition of "relevance." Then at last the National Endowment for the Humanities looked on the Institute, saw that it was good, and awarded it a new, contingent, three-year grant. Battle-scarred but heartened, the committee which proceeded to lay specific plans for the 1974 Institute consisted of the following members:

John M. Headley (UNC-Chapel Hill), Co-chairman
    until January, 1974
Edward P. Mahoney (Duke University)
Jerry L. Mills (UNC-Chapel Hill)
Philip A. Stadter (UNC-Chapel Hill)
David C. Steinmetz (Duke University)
Petrus W. Tax (UNC-Chapel Hill)
Bruce W. Wardropper (Duke University)
Siegfried Wenzel (UNC-Chapel Hill), Co-chairman
    after January, 1974
George W. Williams (Duke University)
and myself

Brochures describing the 1974 Institute were distributed in September of 1973, at which time applications from prospective

Fellows were invited. In December, 1973, the selection of Fellows by the Committee was completed, and the Institute itself convened on the Duke University campus in Durham from 15 July to 23 August 1974. The session consisted of six seminars, each with an enrollment of from six to nine Fellows, and each led by a Senior Fellow.[1]

In addition to leading his seminar, each Senior Fellow presented a lecture which was open both to Institute members and to the general public. It is these lectures which constitute the present book. All but one. In subsequent months the lively lecture by Professor William S. Heckscher on "The Ceremonial Staff as an Attribute" continued to grow—not unlike Marvell's vegetable love—until finally, to our mutual regret, it assumed such imposing proportions as to preclude its printing here.

A foreword is properly a place for thanks, and I am pleased to record here my gratitude not only to the National Endowment for the Humanities and the many participants who helped the 1974 Institute *en cours*, but also to a patient committee, to two understanding co-chairmen, and especially to a university administration which, in the persons of Chancellor John O. Blackburn and Provost Frederic N. Cleaveland, stood staunch and helpful through our darkest night. Further thanks are due to our secretaries: first, Mrs. Shirley B. Colton, who worked for the Institute until its opening in July; and, second, Miss Madolene Stone, who stepped in to serve from that time until the present. Finally, thanks go to two Duke graduate students who contributed significantly in various ways: Mr. Gary P. Lehmann and Mr. James H. Quinlan.

The volume at hand, which records a series of lectures so as to make them available to a larger public, is obviously not the place to turn for an impartial appraisal of the organization of which they are a part. Moreover, the 1974 session of the Southeastern Institute is past, and the present volume must stand on its own in the series of the Institute's *Proceedings*, while another session unfolds and still another takes shape on the drawing board. Nevertheless, it may not be amiss to convey our pride and hope in the continuing belief which underlies both the Institute and its publications. Though sometimes it seems that the world has crumbled out again to its atoms, we continue to believe that humanistic studies are, in themselves, of intrinsic concern to the maintenance of learning in a sophisticated nation, and that, among such studies, specialized scholarship in all fields of the Middle Ages and Renaissance is essential— essential to the understanding and retention of that Western heritage of which the humanities are both a part and a result. It is hard to keep the statement from sounding grandiose and complex, but its underlying facts are simple enough and permanently true. Fortuitously, from time to time, they even appear to be relevant.

July, 1975   D. R.
Durham, N.C.   Chairman, 1969–1974

1. The names of all the seminars and their participants are recorded in the appendix of this volume.

Contents

Foreword   v

 I *The Medieval Marriage Market*
      by David Herlihy   3

 II *Vices, Virtues, and Popular Preaching*
      by Siegfried Wenzel   28

 III *The Popular Dimension of the Reformation: An*
      Essay in Methodology and Historiography
      by Hans J. Hillerbrand   55

 IV *Problems in Editing Sixteenth- and Seventeenth-*
      Century Letters
      by Giles E. Dawson   87

 V *Vital and Artistic Structures in the Life of*
      Don Quixote
      by Juan Bautista Avalle-Arce   104

Appendix: List of Seminars and Participants   122

MEDIEVAL
AND
RENAISSANCE STUDIES

I

The Medieval Marriage Market

David Herlihy
Harvard University

In the medieval world, as in most human societies, the terms of marriage normally included conveyances of property between the bride and groom, or their respective families.[1] Assignments of property at marriage served many important functions. Gifts from the groom to the bride's family may at one time have compensated that family for the loss of a daughter, but even the earliest medieval records preserve only fleeting glimpses of a true brideprice.[2] These marital conveyances primarily served to cement the marriage and to help the newly formed household in its principal functions—the rearing of children and the support of its members.

Medieval commentators on marriage repeatedly stressed the symbolic importance of the marital gifts. In the ninth century, for example, Pope Nicholas I referred to the wedding ring, given by the groom to his bride and accepted by her, as a pledge of their fidelity.[3] The conveyance of gifts required witnesses and usually generated written instruments, which served as proof of marriage. The medieval Church, waging constant war against concubinage and casual sexual liaisons, insisted that marriages be publicly announced; governments, too, had evident interest in promoting stable unions and in maintaining clear lines of descent and inheritance. Gifts, publicly conveyed on occasion of marriage, helped endow the new union with public recognition and approval—basic requirements for legitimate matrimony. "Nullum sine dote fiat coniugium"—"let there be no marriage without a marriage gift."[4] This injunction, apparently dating from the Carolingian age, implied that cohabitation of a man and woman, in which no gifts were publicly given or exchanged, was not a licit marriage at all, but concubinage.

On a more substantive level, the conveyance or exchange of gifts gave to the partners a material stake in the permanence of their union. Characteristically in medieval law, the unfaithful spouse, called to justice by his or her partner, lost all claim to the property he or she had given or acquired on occasion of their marriage. Finally, these marital gifts normally involved a settlement of property upon the bride and groom by their respective families. These gifts were thus an anticipated inheritance.[5] All societies, always balancing themselves between deaths and births, must arrange for the orderly transmission of wealth across generations. Along with formal inheritance, the matrimonial gifts were a principal means by which the old transferred wealth to the young, facilitated their marriages, and thus helped assure the survival of their community and culture. The wealth so conveyed formed, in whole or in part, the capital upon which the new family depended, in order to sustain the *onera matrimonii*, the "burdens of matrimony," in the language of Roman law. This same household capital further promised some security to the surviving partner when death took his or her spouse and the marriage was dissolved. The need of the new household for initial capital also gave to the older generation an effective means of controlling who among the young should marry, and when. Control of marriage could be used either to encourage or to repress the growth of population. Medieval societies did not reproduce themselves blindly.

What were the principal terms of marriage in the Middle Ages, affecting property? Who bore the chief burden of investment in the new household, the relatives of the bride or those of the groom? And what factors determined the costs of a medieval marriage? These are the broad questions to which we shall address ourselves in this paper. They are important questions. The terms of marriage, in affecting the transference of property across the generations, helped mold the relationships between parents and children. These terms were also intimately connected with the functions of both men and women in the medieval household and society, the advantages they enjoyed, the

[4]

burdens they bore. In discussing property and marriage we treat, to be sure, a vast topic, but we hope at least to show its implications for many other aspects of medieval social history.

We must begin our rapid survey with a brief, backward glance at one of the parent civilizations of the medieval world, the Roman empire in its classical epoch, from the time of August Caesar until the third century after Christ. In classical Roman law, the principal and for long the only recognized conveyance of property on occasion of marriage was the *dos*, the dowry in modern usage, a donation made by the bride, or on her behalf, to the groom.[6] The *dos* became the property of the husband, but, much as a trustee, he had to administer it in the interests of his wife, and he or his heirs had to account for it when the marriage was dissolved. From the third century A.D. this Roman dotal system was transformed; a new form of marital conveyance appeared alongside the *dos* and gained greatly in relative importance during the period of the late empire. This was a gift conveyed by the groom, or on his behalf, to his bride, a kind of reverse or counter-dowry.[7] In its earliest appearances it is called either the *donatio ante nuptias* or the *sponsalitia largitas*; then, in the Justinian code of the sixth century, it acquired what would be thereafter its standard name: the *donatio propter nuptias*.

Justinian himself, following the example of earlier emperors, stipulated that for a marriage to be legitimate, the *dos* and *donatio* had to be equal, and that all special pacts or agreements made in regard to one should apply equally to the other. Both bride and groom, in other words, or their lineages, were expected to contribute equal shares to the capital of the new household. Here Justinian was apparently legislating against a strong tendency for the reverse dowry to grow, while the bride's contribution, the traditional *dos*, was declining to negligible amounts. In 458, for example, the Emperor Majoran condemned the cupidity of brides and their families, which was allegedly devouring the substance of young men eager for marriage.[8] Some women were apparently paying their dowries from the *donatio* received from their husbands, and thus they contributed effectively nothing to the capital of the new household. These fraudulent practices, pursued at the expense of grooms and sons-in-law, apparently obstructed weddings and reduced the birth rate, which Majoran and other emperors hoped to promote.[9]

Clearly a remarkable shift was occurring in the terms of Roman marriage across the period of the late empire. The eager grooms, once favored by classical law, now were forced to pay substantially for a bride, so much so that the emperors tried to intervene, to protect the interests of the exploited young men.

The growing importance of the reverse dowry under the late empire brought Roman practice much closer to that of the barbarian peoples, the Germans and Celts, who were then threatening and soon penetrating the imperial frontiers. In his famous description of the Germans, written probably in A.D. 98, Tacitus remarked in evident surprise that among the Germans the groom brought the dowry to his bride, not the bride to the groom, as in the practice of classical Rome.[10] These marital gifts among the barbarians took many complex forms, which we shall not review in detail here.[11] But we should observe that according to the barbarian law codes and penitentials, largely redacted between the sixth and ninth centuries, the groom commonly conveyed his gifts directly to the bride and not to her family.[12] His act closely resembles the Roman *donatio propter nuptias*. Like the Roman *donatio*, the barbarian marital gifts also show a tendency to inflate in value, and like the emperors, the barbarian rulers were concerned to place an upward limit on the amount of property conveyed from groom to bride. In Frankish custom, for example, the groom could assign to his bride no more than one-third of his possessions, and his gift therefore came to be called the *tertia*.[13] In 717 the Lombard King Liutprand similarly limited the size of the wedding gift to one-fourth of the groom's property, whence the name *quarta*, thereafter applied to the reverse dowry in Lombard traditions.[14] Although Romans and barbarians followed different systems of law and customs, the outlines of a similar evolution in marital practices seem unmistakable. Across the period of the late empire and into the early Middle Ages, the groom or his lineage was persuaded or forced to assume a principal share of the costs of marriage. So complete is this evolution, or revolution, that in the Latin West explicit references to the Roman *dos* virtually disappear from the documents.[15] In the early medieval marriage, it was the groom who paid.

In 866 Pope Nicholas I explained to the Bulgarians how marriages were contracted in the West, that is, among those peoples professing Latin Christianity. "Our people," he states,

both men and women, when they make a marriage agreement, do not wear bands of gold, silver, or other metal, upon their brows. Rather, with the consent of the contracting parties and of those in whose authority they are, a betrothal is plighted, which is a promise of future marriage. As a pledge of faith, the groom betroths the bride by giving her a ring. The groom also conveys to her, by written instrument in the presence of witnesses summoned by both parties, a *dos* which both parties have agreed upon. Shortly after this, or at a suitable time, lest it appear that the act was done before the time prescribed by law, the two are brought to the marriage contracts. . . .[16]

Pope Nicholas, it should be noted, makes no mention whatsoever of any dowry or gift made by the bride to her husband. This important text was included in Gratian's *Decretum*, redacted about 1140, the most influential collection of canons yet to be made in the Latin Church. The long period between the decline of Roman rule and the middle twelfth century was the golden age of the reverse dowry in the Western marriage.

From approximately the twelfth century, European society experienced many fundamental, apparently accelerating changes; those changes once more touched and transformed the basic terms of marriage in the West. From the early decades of the twelfth century, the documents for the first time since antiquity make direct reference to the *dos* in its Roman sense, to the true dowry.[17] Sometime about 1140, in what is probably the earliest surviving medieval tract devoted to the dowry, the jurist Martin Gosia restated Justinian's position, that in a legitimate marriage the mutual contributions of bride and groom, or their respective families, had to be equal.[18] Later decretists and decretalists—commentators on the basic law collections of the medieval Church—reiterate that a dowry, at least equal to the groom's gift, was essential for legitimate marriage.[19]

The acts of notaries working in the Italian port city of Genoa, dating from 1155, give us our oldest, full picture of actual marriage agreements in western Europe. The marriage agreements contained in the oldest surviving chartulary, that of Giovanni Scriba, redacted from 1155 to 1164, show that in most instances the contributions of bride and groom to the new household were in fact equal.[20]

But equality was not long maintained. The changes in the terms of marriage are most easily discernible in Italy, a land rich in both private acts and legislative enactments. From the middle twelfth century, the governments of the Italian cities moved to limit the claims of wives upon their husbands' property. In 1143 the commune of Genoa abolished the *tertia*, the right of a wife to one-third of the household property after the death of her husband, according to the Frankish custom followed in the city. An illustration in the pages of a contemporary chronicle shows two women of Genoa weeping over their lost advantage.[21] Genoa at the same time decreed that the reverse dowry should never exceed one-fourth the value of the true dowry, and should at all events never surpass one hundred pounds of Genoese money. Alexandria in 1179, Volterra in 1200, Florence in 1253, and other cities imposed similar limits, both relative and absolute, on the groom's contribution to the marriage, in relation to the bride's.[22] The spirit behind this campaign is colorfully expressed by a phrase used several times in a Milanese customary dated 1216: the *odium quartae*, the hatred of the wife's traditional claim in Lombard law to one-quarter of her husband's property as her marriage gift.[23]

In Italy, too, the individual marriage agreements, preserved by the thousands in notarial chartularies, record in detail the decline of the reverse dowry to virtual insignificance by the fourteenth century, and the corresponding shift of the costs of marriage to the side of the bride. At Genoa, already in the years

1200 to 1211, according to the marriage agreements redacted by the notary Giovanni di Guiberto, the bride usually brought more wealth into the marriage than did her husband.[24]

The terms of marriage were completely transformed in Italy between the twelfth and the fourteenth centuries. In the early fourteenth century Dante remarked in his *Divine Comedy* that the size of dowries was exceeding all reasonable measure, and he hearkened back to those better times, in the eleventh and twelfth centuries, when the birth of a daughter did not strike terror into her father's heart.[25] All our records support the truth and the force of his observation.

Outside of Italy the profusion of local customs, their instability, and the limited number of surviving marriage agreements make this evolution difficult to follow, but there are many indications that the treatment of women in marriage was deteriorating from the late twelfth century. In their history of English law, Pollock and Maitland conclude that the rise of the feudal order, which closely linked tenure with military service, inevitably curtailed the rights and claims of widows and other women.[26] In the thirteenth century the English woman lost all capacity to own chattels or movables, which at her marriage passed completely under the ownership of her husband.[27] Analogous changes can be found elsewhere in Europe. In some regions the dower, the portion of the husband's property assigned to his bride at marriage, at one time gave to the widow full ownership over the portion at the death of her husband, but later was considered to confer only a right of lifetime usufruct.[28] In 1205, at the request of his French vassals, King John of England declared that widows could no longer claim one-half the acquisitions made by their households while their marriages endured, but were to be content with their dowers.[29] The goal of all these complex and admittedly often obscure changes seems to have been to limit acquisition of property by women through marriage gifts or any other means.

How are we to explain these striking shifts in the terms of Western marriage, evident at the very start of the Middle Ages and again from the late twelfth century? Here we shall direct our attention principally to Italy, where these changes are most easily tracked in the abundant surviving sources.

Superficially viewed, the decline and virtual disappearance of the true dowry under the late empire might be regarded as a substitution of barbarian for Roman practices, and thus considered a consequence of the barbarian conquests. But as we have already noted, properly within the tradition of Roman law, properly among the subjects of the empire, the position of the groom was deteriorating in late antiquity. So also, the revival of the true dowry from the twelfth century cannot be exclusively attributed to the renaissance of Roman legal studies, which was simultaneously occurring in the medieval schools. The new jurisprudence brought clarity and accuracy to the legal records, but the erudition of a few scholars could hardly have transformed the basic terms of marriage. The medieval jurists were the interpreters, not the architects, of the new social realities.

These transformations in the terms of the Western marriage have also been associated with changes in the basic character of the economy, specifically with the decline of commercial exchange in late antiquity and its revival from about the twelfth century.[30] According to this view, in a commercial or monetized economy the *paterfamilias* had to concentrate large sums of liquid capital, and he needed freedom to manage them. The system of the reverse dowry gave the wife not only a claim to a substantial portion of the husband's capital, but also a voice in its administration. The necessity of securing the wife's agreement to commercial transactions allegedly obstructed the managerial freedom of the household head and impeded commercial progress. This mattered little when the economy remained preeminently agrarian—across the early Middle Ages—but was supposedly incompatible with expanding commerce and industry from the twelfth century.

In truth, however, it is hard to see how the dotal system could have decisively favored commercial revival. The hidden assumption here is that women were incompetent to make or to participate in commercial decisions. But in our earliest large collection of commercial records, those of the city of Genoa, women frequently appear as investors or participants in business ventures, with no evident damage to trade. The dotal system further forced the *paterfamilias* to commit large sums of his needed capital to the marriage of his daughters. The lure of dowries probably also turned some young men into dowry hunters, diverting their energies from more productive enterprises. There is, to be sure, a chronological correspondence between the withering of the monetized economy of antiquity and the disappearance of the Roman dowry, and between the commercial revival of the central Middle Ages and the dowry's return. But the connections between these two parallel movements are unclear, and even the existence of direct links far from certain.

The shifts in the terms of marriage have also been associated with supposed changes in the fundamental character of the Western household.[31] The barbarian and early medieval household was supposedly an agnatic association, that is, based on male descent, which managed its patrimony collectively. The barbarian *paterfamilias*, it has been argued, was not free to alienate part of the household property for the benefit of daughters, and therefore could not grant a dowry. The Roman dotal system thus disappeared, as it could not survive when the patrimony was collectively owned and managed in the interests of the males. Supposedly the return of the dowry came with the dissolution of the collective character of the barbarian household, the triumph of individualistic principles of property ownership, and the improved treatment of women.

But this picture of the early medieval family seems to be largely mythical. Thousands of land sales and exchanges are extant from the centuries when the reverse dowry predominated, and it is rarely possible to discern the family functioning as a collective unit. If the patrimony of the household was collectively managed and indivisible for benefit of women, how could the groom promise, and his heirs subsequently deliver, one-third or one-fourth his patrimony to his wife, then widow? Under such conditions, no system of marital conveyances could have functioned. In fact no theoretical conception of the nature of the medieval household is likely to explain these changes in the terms of marriage, as those changes essentially reflect the external relationships of families or lineages, not their internal structures.

We are left without a convincing explanation for these shifts in the basic terms of the Western marriage, and it may be that the large gaps in our sources will never allow us to find a fully satisfactory answer. But there also seems to be one other factor operative here which so far has not attracted the direct attention of scholars: the character of the medieval marriage market. What do we mean by a marriage market? If a man or woman wished to marry, he or she, or someone on his or her behalf, had to meet certain costs, the size of which was subject to negotiation. Of course, religious beliefs, values, customs, and the like played a role of major importance in marriage arrangements, as they largely defined who was eligible for marriage, who was desirable as a partner, and how courtship should be pursued. Public laws also frequently intervened, setting, for example, minimum or maximum limits to the size of the marriage gifts. But at all times both custom and law left considerable scope for a system of bidding and response, for market interactions, in sum. In the Middle Ages, to be sure, the true agents operating on this market were usually not individual men and women, but families and lineages, with sons and daughters to marry. Within the limits set by religion, custom, and law, these families wished to see their sons and daughters married under the most advantageous terms they could obtain. This simple, nearly self-evident principle is all that the concept of a marriage market fundamentally implies.

What determined the negotiating strength of a medieval family, seeking to arrange the marriage of a son or daughter? The beauty, the health, the social connections of the young man or woman are the most obvious considerations. But one other, less immediately evident factor was also operative: the relative numbers of men and of women actively seeking a mate. If, for example, more men are seeking brides than there are brides to be had, three results will follow. The desired girls will marry under terms favorable to themselves or to their families; the men who marry will have to meet those terms at high cost; and some men will be priced out of the market. Such is the common pattern which systems of bidding and response usually produce.

It is of course true that at birth the numbers of male and female babies show approximate equality, but this biological fact does not guarantee that there will be equal numbers of brides seeking grooms and grooms seeking brides when the babies grow to marital age. One or the other of the sexes may endure higher mortalities during childhood, reflecting different standards of nourishment or treatment in the household. Different functional responsibilities, as, for example, military services demanded from young men, may also affect relative rates of survival and tip the balance between the sexes at age of marriage. Of particular importance is a cultural or social consideration: the willingness or reluctance to marry, or, on the part of families, to allow their offspring to marry, at a certain age. If families, for example, seek to retain at home their bachelor sons for a longer period than their daughters, this policy will flood the marriage market with supernumerary, nubile girls; weaken their negotiating position; and force many who marry to enter the marital state on unfavorable terms. Critical in this regard is the mean age of first marriage for men and for women, as it directly measures their willingness or reluctance to marry, or of their families to allow their marriages. Particularly under conditions of high mortalities, if men marry substantially later in life than do women, fewer males will ever actively seek a bride, as some will die before reaching the preferred age of first marriage. This erosion of the ranks of prospective grooms will mean that some of the younger girls will have no chance of finding a husband, and that all the younger girls will be forced to seek husbands upon an unfavorable market.

If this analysis has merit, then the triumph of the reverse dowry in the early Middle Ages—the favorable terms, in other words, with which women entered upon marriage—implies that there was a relative shortage of nubile girls, in relation to men seeking mates, on the marriage market. We have several indications, both direct and indirect, that eligible men did indeed outnumber nubile women in early medieval society. The earliest surviving records which illuminate the balance of sexes in medieval communities are Carolingian manorial surveys, dating from the late eighth and ninth centuries. They characteristically show a preponderance of males throughout the population. The largest of these surveys describes the estates of the monastery of Saint-Germain des Prés near Paris, and indicates that there were upwards of 120 males per 100 females upon the monastic lands.[32] These surveys are limited to the peasant population, and there are grounds for doubting their precision. But the consistency with which they indicate a male preponderance is telling evidence that women were in short supply in the early medieval world.

The barbarian legal codes give indirect evidence of the same phenomenon. The codes measure a person's social worth by assigning to him or her a wergild, a fine to be paid to relatives should he or she be killed or injured. Women were clearly valued in barbarian society. In the law of the Salian Franks, the free woman was protected by the same wergild, two hundred solidi, as the free man. But during her child-bearing years, which obviously included her nubile years, her wergild was tripled to six hundred solidi, the same sum assigned to the elite of society, the followers of the king or the bishops.[33] The law of the Alemanni gives double the value to free women, compared with free men, at every age.[34] Perhaps most remarkable is the protection the codes extend at times to female infants. In the law of the Alemanni, if a pregnant woman is so injured that she aborts the fetus, then the fine is twelve solidi. But if the fetus can be identified as female, the fine is doubled.[35] The law of the Salian Franks contains a similar provision, and here the wergild assigned to an aborted female fetus is apparently even more than double the sum given for an aborted male.[36]

There is also evidence, sparse but extant, that the early medieval marriage was on occasion matrilocal, that is, the newly married couple came to live with the bride's family rather than the groom's—a practice rarely encountered in European communities from the late Middle Ages. In a ninth-century survey of the serfs belonging to the monastery of Saint-Victor of Marseilles, the number of women remaining with their families of origin after marrying so-called "foreign men" is larger than the number of men in the households married to "foreign women."[37] One is here reminded of Charlemagne's own renowned attachment to his daughters, his refusal to let them depart from his entourage. This suggests that women were valued in the early medieval household, and that efforts were made to retain daughters even after marriage. It is worth noting—still according to our Carolingian surveys—that the richer the household, the more women it was likely to contain.[38] To live comfortably in the early Middle Ages apparently required that women be present in the household in significant numbers. We also have hints that the apparent shortage of nubile girls and the high reverse dowries demanded meant that some impoverished males could not marry at all.[39]

Finally, our admittedly scanty data indicate that ages at first marriage were approximately equal for brides and for grooms, but that the brides were not especially young and were at times even older than their grooms. We would expect a pattern of delayed first marriage for women in a society in which women performed valuable services for their families of origin. The ninth-century survey of the estates of Saint-Victor of Marseilles identifies marriageable men and women in the community, who are called *baccalarii* and *baccalarie*. Their numbers are relatively large, constituting about a quarter of the entire population, which would indicate a considerable delay between puberty and first marriage.[40] Their numbers are also nearly equal for both sexes, suggesting equality of the ages of bride and groom when marriage was eventually contracted. However, in 731 the Lombard King Liutprand complained that "adult and already mature women" were marrying boys who had not yet reached legitimate age.[41] He decreed that no woman should attempt to marry a boy until he reached age thirteen. This law is the exact reversal of enactments we encounter in the Italian cities from the thirteenth century, which sought to prevent the marriage of underaged girls rather than boys.[42] The society of Lombard Italy was far different from the society which becomes visible in the same land from about the year 1200.

Our earliest fairly extensive information on ages of first marriage seems to survive only from the twelfth century. A papal decretal of 1185–87 mentions, at Pisa, a girl of twelve married to a boy of nine or ten; in another decretal a girl of seven is cited as married to a boy of six.[43] These unions were obviously not yet consummated, but we may conclude that marriages of older brides to younger grooms were still not uncommon in Italy of the twelfth century.

The Genoese notarial chartularies of the same period show further evidence of this. In 1156, for example, a husband and wife sell a piece of land, and the husband alone promises to confirm the sale when he reaches legitimate age, here presumably twenty-five.[44] In this marriage, the husband was certainly younger than his wife, although in other records either the wife alone or both spouses appear as underaged. In twelfth-century Genoa, a rough equality in the ages of the spouses seems to have been the rule, but an older wife married to a younger husband was not unknown.

This, then, is how we would describe the state of the marriage market in the early Middle Ages. Nubile girls were in relatively short supply and were much valued in their families of origin. They were not exceptionally young at first marriage, but were normally equal in age to, although sometimes older than, their grooms. The grooms had to compete for these numerically fewer and appreciated women, and this generated and maintained inflationary pressures on the reverse dowries they had to pay.

The fact that girls were so much valued both by their families of origin and by their prospective husbands suggests that their numbers were comparatively few. We can only speculate upon the reason. In this agrarian society they were valued in large part for the work they could perform, not only in household service or in making cloth—doubtless their chief functions among the wealthy—but also in agricultural labors. In

Tacitus' depiction of Germanic society, women and children were chiefly responsible for the *domus officia*, the labors needed to support the household, while even the common freemen gave themselves largely to idleness.[45] The strenuous physical demands upon women may have taken a heavy toll as they aged. Moreover, in a disordered society, the economic value of women as workers made them the frequent victims of abduction and enslavement, to which we have frequent reference in the barbarian codes and penitentials. Women were valued in early medieval society, but the functions which gave them their worth may also have undermined their chances for survival.

This pattern changes dramatically from the late twelfth century. Women become relatively more numerous in medieval society, at least within the feudal aristocracy and in the growing towns. An English survey, the *Rotuli de dominabus*, dated 1185, allows us to judge the distribution of the sexes within one distinctive but we hope representative segment of the Anglo-Norman nobility.[46] The document lists the possessions and the children of noble widows, whom the English king holds within his power to give in marriage. The ages of the widows range between eighteen and seventy, and of course many of their offspring were already mature. Among the offspring, women distinctly outnumber men, by 155 to 138. The reasons for this seem apparent. In a social group given to warfare, young men faced greater occupational hazards than young women. At the same time, the establishment of stable principalities and the spread of chivalrous ideals at least partially exonerated women from the risks of warfare.

Urban conditions also seem to have favored the survival of women. The thirteenth-century scholastic Albertus Magnus once wrote that women live longer than men, and the principal reason he gave for this is that "they work less and are not so much consumed."[47] Teaching and writing in cities, he doubtlessly had urban women foremost in mind, and in urban economies women no longer fulfilled the exacting but essential labors they had assumed on the farms of the early Middle Ages. This exoneration from heavy physical labor may have lengthened the days of the urban woman, but it also reduced her contribution to and limited her economic value for her family. Finally, still broader changes in the medieval cultural ethos may have benefited women. It may be that, like warfare itself, hard physical labor was coming to be regarded as inappropriate for women.

If women survived better, they also, somewhat paradoxically, married younger. The *Rotuli de dominabus* shows that many of these aristocratic ladies were in their late teens when they married.[48] The Lady Alda, for example, must have been less than fourteen when she married, as her eldest child was sixteen when she was only thirty.[49] Moreover, to judge from saints' lives, in both the Flemish and the Italian towns the age of first marriage for girls at about the year 1200 seems also to have been between thirteen and sixteen years.[50]

At the same time, our sources point to a marked and growing reluctance on the part of males to take a wife, particularly within the feudal aristocracy and the bourgeoisie.[51] In that bizarre twelfth-century Latin poem *The Complaint of Nature*, by Alain of Lille, marriage itself appears as an allegorical figure in tattered garments, to complain that males are avoiding its services in preference for other, less wholesome sexual outlets; nature herself observes that women (the natural anvils) are bewailing the absence of hammers (that is, men) and sadly demanding them.[52]

From the late twelfth century, at least in the medieval aristocracies, girls were usually still in their teens at first marriage, while men often postponed marriage until their late twenties or thirties.[53] In the late medieval French satire, the *Fifteen Joys of Marriage*, the wife complains to her obviously older husband that her wedding dress has become too short for her, as she has continued to grow since her marriage.[54]

The reluctance of males to marry in the late Middle Ages reduced their numbers on the marriage market and destroyed the advantages which women had formerly enjoyed in seeking husbands. In Dante's image, the *paterfamilias*, panicked by the dismal prospect of attracting a groom, tried to marry off his daughter as quickly as possible, even when she was unreasonably young and the dowry remained unreasonably high.[55] The desperation to place one's daughters, as well as the declining economic value of the girl within the household, probably explain the low age at first marriage for women in the late Middle Ages.

Why did men, from approximately the late twelfth century, postpone marriage? A critical factor here seems to have been the effort to protect the family patrimony from excessive parcelization among heirs. In the early Middle Ages, when population levels were low, violence endemic, and survival rates poor, families seem not to have feared a surplus of heirs. By the late twelfth century, however, under conditions of a growing population and diminishing opportunities for the sons close to home, the family seems to have turned inward upon its patrimony, conserved it as an essential prop to its power, and prevented its disintegration through excessive partitionings.[56] In the cities, too, the need on the part of males to acquire experience and skill in the arts of trade and to nurture their capital also discouraged and delayed marriage.

Late first marriage for men and early first marriage for women transformed the terms of matrimony in the late Middle Ages, in forcing the fathers of nubile girls to engage in competitive bidding to attract reluctant grooms. With such conditions prevailing on the marriage market, it is understandable that the costs of the new union should have shifted primarily to the bride and her family, the reverse dowry should have declined, and the true dowry or *dos* should have become the principal conveyance of property associated with marriage.

The young age of first marriage for women and the relatively advanced age for men had at least one other important social effect. In spite of the risks of childbirth, wives had a good chance of surviving their husbands. Still young as widows, they were in excellent position to block the transmission of the family patrimony, in whole or in part, to the younger generation. In traditional India under seemingly comparable conditions, the devoted widow or suttee was expected to immolate herself upon her husband's pyre—a personal sacrifice which also conveniently freed the family property for transmission to the younger generation.[57] In medieval Europe governments and families could only limit the widow's claims upon the property of her husband and restrict her capacity to acquire or to manage other possessions. In the middle twelfth century the Statutes of Pisa already complain that "mothers, in demanding [return of] the dowry and the reverse dowry from their sons, more often than not show not maternal affection but a step-mother's lack of familial feeling."[58] "The female sex," reads a commonplace of the legal literature, "is most avaricious and most tenacious and more eager to receive than to give."[59] In the late sixteenth century, the commune of Correggio in Italy tried to restrict acquisitions by women "for the public good and for the conservation of families and of male lines, which are often ruined by the excessive bequests and donations which daily are made to women, without having regard to the conservation of the male line."[60]

Under the late medieval system of marriage, the wife or widow found herself in a paradoxical situation. Much younger than her husband, much closer in age than he to their children, she was in a position to serve as an intermediary between the generations of fathers and sons. But here her young age at first marriage and subsequent longevity also made her an obstacle to the transmission of property from fathers to children, and earned for her the *odium* for her claims to which the Milanese customary refers. Perhaps her long-lasting claims upon the property of her deceased husband and children can partially explain the campaign—everywhere apparent in the Europe of the late Middle Ages—to limit her rights.

These, then, are the two most visible faces of marriage which our sources allow us to see in the Middle Ages. The terms of marriage as they affected property were transformed about the year 1200. The European marriage, household, and family were thus starkly different in the late medieval centuries from what they had been before. Although this survey has been rapid, I hope at least to have shown the broad implications of this topic for medieval social history. The lives of most medieval people were lived out within or in close association with marriage. The study of medieval social history may appropriately take marriage as a central and advantageous point of departure.

Notes

1. I would like to express my gratitude to Professor Diane Hughes of Victoria College, the University of Toronto, for allowing me to read in advance of publication her article "Marriage Settlements, Families, and Women in the Cities of Medieval Italy." The article contains a rich bibliography of studies on marital conveyances in Italy during the Middle Ages.

Useful published studies of the marital gifts in medieval laws and practices are the following: Franco Ercole, "Vicende storiche della dote romana nella pratica medievale dell'Italia superiore," *Archivio Giuridico* (henceforth, *AG*), 80 (1908), 393–490, and 81 (1908), 34–148; Francesco Brandileone, "Studi preliminari sullo svolgimento storico dei rapporti patrimoniali fra coniugi in Italia," *Scritti di storia del diritto privato italiano*, ed. G. Ermini (Bologna, 1931), I, 231–319; *idem*, "Sulla storia e la natura della *donatio propter nuptias*," *Scritti di storia del diritto privato italiano*, I, 119–228; André Lemaire, "La Dotatio de l'épouse de l'époque mérovingienne au XIIIe siècle," *Revue Historique de Droit Français et Etranger* (henceforth, *RHDFE*), 4th ser. 8 (1929), 569–580; *idem*, "Les Origines de la communauté de biens entre époux dans le droit coutumier français," *RHDFE*, 4th ser. 7 (1929), 584–643; Manuel Paulo Merêa, "O dote nos documentos dos seculos IX–XII," *Estudos de direito hispânico medieval*, I (Coimbra, 1952), 59–150; Gabriel Lepointe, *Droit romain et ancien droit français. Régimes matrimoniaux, libéralités, successions* (Paris, 1958); Gerda Merschberger, *Die Rechtsstellung der germanischen Frau* (Leipzig, 1937).

2. On the primitive brideprice, its character, and its relation to the marital gifts, see Heinrich Brunner, *Deutsche Rechtsgeschichte* (Leipzig, 1887), I, 95; and S. Kalifa, "Singularités matrimoniales chez les anciens Germains: Le Rapt et le droit de la femme à disposer d'elle-même," *RHDFE*, 4th ser. 48 (1970), 199–225.

3. For the text, see below, n. 16.

4. The text apparently first appears in the False Decretals. See Lemaire, "Dotatio de l'épouse," p. 569.

5. On the close relation between inheritance systems and marriage settlements, see Jack Goody and S. J. Tambiah, *Bridewealth and Dowry* (Cambridge, 1973); Jean Yver, *Egalité entre héritiers et exclusion des enfants dotés. Essai de géographie coutumière* (Paris, 1966).

6. W. W. Buckland, *A Manual of Roman Private Law* (2nd ed.; Cambridge, 1947), pp. 64–67; Max Kaser, *Das römische Privatrecht* (Handbuch der Altertumswissenschaft, X, 3, 3; Munich, 1955), I, 284–290.

7. Kaser, *Das römische Privatrecht* (Munich, 1959), II, 134–141. Legal historians generally associate the rise of the *donatio* with Eastern influences. Before Justinian's time the gift had to be conveyed before marriage (whence the name *ante nuptias*) as Roman law forbade gifts between spouses. Justinian himself excepted the *donatio* from that prohibition.

8. *Leges novellae ad Theodosianum pertinentes*, ed. T. Mommsen and Paul M. Meyer (2nd ed.; Berlin, 1954), p. 166. "Sane quoniam quorundam cupiditatibus obviandum est, qui generorum exhauriunt facultates ac sibi vel filiabus suis vel subornatis . . . ab incautis iuvenibus et futuri coniugii desiderio concitatis multa faciunt occulta fraude conferri. . . ."

9. *Leges novellae*, p. 165: "Et quia studiose tractatur a nobis utilitas filiorum, quos et numerosius procreari pro Romani nominis optamus augmento. . . ." For further comment on what one historian calls the "forte tendenza" for women under the late empire to bring no dowry at all, or a small one, to their marriages, see Ercole, "Vicende storiche," *AG*, 80 (1908), 431.

10. "Dotem non uxor marito, sed uxori maritus offert," *Germania*, cap. 18; see H. Mattingly, *Tacitus on Britain and Germany: A Translation of the "Agricola" and the "Germania"* (Baltimore, 1967), p. 115.

11. The studies of Brandileone and Ercole, cited in n. 1 above, contain extensive discussions of the technical character of these gifts.

12. For the Irish penitentials, see Ludwig Bieler, *The Irish Penitentials* (Scriptores Latini Hiberniae, V: Dublin, 1963). The early "Synodus I S. Patricii," cap. 22 (p. 56), makes it appear that the bride's father received the *dos*. "Si quis tradiderit filiam suam viro . . . et acceperit dotem. . . ." But according to later penitentials, the groom's gift went to the bride. See the "Welsh canons," cap. 47 (p. 144), "Si quis filiam marito tradiderit, legitimam dotem accipiat. . . ." The editor construes "he" (that is, the father) to be the subject of "accipiat," but the sense of the entire passage seems to require "she" (that is, the bride). The passage goes on to state under what conditions the dowry might pass to the father, and would make no sense if the father had already received it ("Quod si hos non habuerit, patri dari iubetur. . ."). On traces of a brideprice in Lombard law, specifically in the payment known as the *meta*, see Brandileone, "Rapporti patrimoniali," p. 232. According to Brandileone, in earliest Lombard practice the *meta* was the price paid by the groom to the bride's father for the *mundium*, or jurisdiction, which he held over the girl. Subsequently, however, the *meta* was paid directly to the bride.

13. Brandileone, "Rapporti patrimoniali," p. 246.

14. *Leges langobardorum 643–866*, ed. F. Beyerle (2nd ed.; Witzenhausen, 1962), Liutprandi leges, 7.I, year 717 (p. 102). "Ipsum autem morgingap nolumus ut amplius sit, nisi quarta pars de eius substantia, qui ipsum morgingab fecit." The "morgingap" was the *Morgengabe*, or gift, originally conveyed by the groom to the bride after the consummation of their marriage. It subsequently becomes fused with the *meta* and was paid before the marriage.

15. The fate of the Roman *dos* in the barbarian West has been much discussed. German historians of law have tended to maintain that the Roman dotal system disappeared entirely, but Italian legal historians, especially Brandileone, have successfully found traces at least of the Roman reverse dowry in early medieval Italy. Brandileone ("Rapporti patrimoniali," p. 273) maintains that the *antifactum*, a common name for the reverse dowry in early medieval Italian private acts, was the Roman *donatio propter nuptias*. But all historians of early medieval law, including Brandileone ("Rapporti patrimoniali," p. 265), recognize that the true dowry paid by the bride had lost importance. Ercole, "Vicende storiche," *AG*, 80 (1908), 417, observes that even in those areas of Italy under strong Byzantine influence the reverse dowry ("assegni maritali") was the dominant conveyance between the spouses.

16. *Monumenta Germaniae Historica* (henceforth, *MGH*), Epistolarum Tomi VI, Pars I, *Epistolae Karolini Aevi*, Tomus IV (Berlin, 1902), Epistolae Nicolai I papae, ed. E. Perels, no. 99 (13 Nov. 866), pp. 569–570:

> Nostrates siquidem tam mares quam feminae non ligaturam auream vel argenteam, aut ex quolibet metallo compositam, quando nuptialia foedera contrahunt, in capitibus deferunt, sed post sponsalia, quae futurarum sunt nuptiarum promissa, foedera quaeque consensu eorum qui haec contrahunt, et eorum, in quorum potestate sunt, celebrantur, et postquam arrhis sponsam sibi sponsus per digitum fidei a se annulo insignitum desponderit dotemque utrique placitam sponsus ei cum scripto pactum hoc continente coram invitatis ab utraque parte tradiderit, aut mox aut apto tempore, ne videlicet ante tempus lege diffinitum tale quid fieri presumatur, ambo ad nuptialia foedera perducuntur.

David Herlihy

See also the *Corpus iuris canonici: Editio lipsiensis secunda,* ed. Aemilius Fried-berg (Leipzig, 1879), Pars prior: Decretum magistri Gratiani, Pars II, causa XXX, V, c. 3, Nykolaus ad consulta Bulgarorum.

17. Ercole, "Vicende storiche," *AG,* 81 (1908), 39, places the earliest references to the true *dos* in the first years of the twelfth century, but says that its use is not much diffused until after 1150.

18. "Martini de iure dotium tractatus," in Hermann Kantorowicz, *Studies in the Glossators of the Roman Law: Newly Discovered Writings of the Twelfth Century* (Cambridge, 1938), p. 261: ". . . equalitas enim dotis et propter nuptias donationis eadem esse debet et in augmentis earum omnino exigitur equalitas tam in quantitate quam in partibus, maioribus pactis ad minora deducendis, ut uterque minorem partem lucretur."

19. *Summa domini Henrici Hostiensis* (Lyons, 1542), 219ᵛ, "Qualiter donatio propter nuptias." *Iohannis Andreae i.c. bononiensis In quartum Decretalium librum novella commentaria* (Venice, 1581), p. 68.

20. *Il cartolare di Giovanni Scriba,* ed. Mario Chiaudano and Mattia Moresco (Regesta chartarum Italiae, 19–20; Rome, 1935). According to my count, out of thirty marriage agreements, the dowry is higher than the reverse dowry in ten instances; the reverse dowry is higher in four; and the two are equal in sixteen.

21. *Annali genovesi di Caffaro e de' suoi continuatori dal MXCIX al MCCXCIII,* ed. Luigi Belgrano (Fonti per la storia d'Italia, 11–14 *bis*; Genoa, 1890–1929), I, 31: "in isto consulatu tercie ablate fuerunt mulieribus." This edition also re-produces the sketch of the two weeping women.

22. Brandileone, "Rapporti patrimoniali," p. 273. Ercole, "Vicende storiche," *AG,* 81 (1908), 92–115. *Statuti di Volterra,* ed. Enrico Fiumi, I (Florence, 1951), 5, enactment dated May, 1200, requiring that the *donatio* should be no more than "quartam partem dotis." *Statuti della Repubblica fiorentina,* ed. Romolo Caggese, II: *Statuto del Podestà dell' anno 1325* (Florence, 1921), p. 98, ". . . ut donatio non excedat libras quinquaginta vel quartam bonorum viri," enacted 1253.

23. *Le due edizioni milanese e torinese delle Consuetudini di Milano dell'anno 1216, cenni ed appunti,* ed. Francesco Berlan (Venice, 1872), cap. 17, p. 245, "quarta tamen, propter eius odium, de illis non debetur"; p. 246, ". . . similiter, odio quartae, de nostra consuetudine, quarta non dabitur."

24. *Notai liguri del sec. XII,* 5: *Giovanni di Guiberto (1200–1211),* ed. M. W. Hall-Cole, H. G. Krueger, R. G. Reinert, and R. L. Reynolds (Documenti e studi per la storia del commercio e del diritto commerciale italiano, 17–18; Turin, 1939–40). According to my count, out of forty-one marriage agreements, the dowry is larger than the reverse dowry in twenty-five instances; the reverse dowry is higher in one; and the two are equal in fifteen. See above, n. 20, for the distribu-tion some forty years earlier.

25. "Non faceva, nascendo, ancor paura / la figlia al padre; ché'l tempo e la dote / non fuggien quinci e quindi la misura," *Paradiso,* xv, 103–105. Dante is comparing the simple but virtuous Florentines of former times with the corrupt men of his own day.

26. Sir Frederick Pollock and F. W. Maitland, *The History of English Law before the Time of Edward I* (2nd ed.; Cambridge, 1952), II, 419, "[Feudalism] destroys the equality between husband and wife."

27. Sir William Holdsworth, *A History of English Law* (4th ed.; London, 1935), III, 524.

28. Cf. Lemaire, "Communauté de biens," *RHDFE,* 4th ser. 7 (1929), 627, who concludes that widely in France the dower or *dotalicium* was assigned in full property to the end of the tenth century, but in the twelfth century the dower tended to be limited to a "droit de jouissance viagère."

[24]

29. Cited in *ibid.*, p. 602. The text reads: "quod mulier . . . non capiat ibidem medietatem *de adquisitionibus viri sui* . . . sed suo maritagio sit contenta."

30. Brandileone, "Rapporti patrimoniali," p. 308, stresses the influence exerted by growing commercial fortunes in the towns. For additional discussion, see Manlio Bellomo, *Profili della famiglia italiana nell'età dei comuni* (Catania, 1966), p. 140.

31. Ercole, "Vicende storiche," *AG*, 81 (1908), 71 and 72, lays great stress on the "costituzione famigliare" as a "società economica," maintaining also that "la proprietà famigliare era . . . collettiva."

32. *Polyptyque de l'abbaye de Saint-Germain des Prés*, ed. A. Longnon (2 vols.; Paris, 1895). Among the various estates, the sex ratios for adults ranged from 110.3 to 252.9 men per 100 women. See Emily R. Coleman, "Medieval Marriage Characteristics: A Neglected Factor in the History of Medieval Serfdom," *The Family in History: Interdisciplinary Essays*, ed. Theodore K. Rabb and Robert I. Rotberg (New York, 1973), pp. 1–15.

33. *Lex Salica: 100 Titel-Text*, ed. Karl Eckhardt (Weimar, 1953), cap. 31–33, p. 146. This text assigns a fine of three hundred solidi to the life of a free woman, six hundred solidi if she is in child-bearing years, and two hundred after she is "post media etate." But according to the "septem causas," the "puella ingenua" bore a wergild of two hundred solidi. *Pactus legis Salicae: Kapitularien und 70 Titel Text*, ed. Karl Eckhardt (Berlin and Frankfurt, 1956), pp. 460–461.

34. *Leges Alamannorum*, ed. K. Lehmann (*MGH*, Legum Sectio I. Tomi V, Pars I; Hanover, 1966), cap. 60.2, p. 130: "Feminas autem eorum semper in duplum conponatur."

35. *Ibid.*, cap. 91.1, p. 150.

36. *Pactus legis Salicae*, ed. Eckhardt, Capitulare III, cap. CIV.8, p. 422, "Si vero infans puella est, qui excutetur, MMCCCC solidos conponat." If the dead fetus was male, apparently the fine was only six hundred solidi, and nine hundred if the woman also died. The text is not clear, but it may be that the woman and her female fetus who bore the extraordinary wergild of 2,400 solidi were under the special protection of the king.

37. The foreign spouses are called "extranei" or "extranee." *Cartulaire de l'abbaye de Saint-Victor de Marseille*, ed. Benjamin Guérard (Paris, 1857), II, 633–656. For further comment see Stephen Weinberger, "Peasant Households in Provence: ca. 800–1100," *Speculum*, 48 (1973), 247–257; and my own article, "Life Expectancies for Women in Medieval Society," in *The Role of Women in the Middle Ages*, ed. Rosemarie Thee Morewedge (Albany, 1975), pp. 1–22.

38. Emily R. Coleman notes the tendency for women to be found in the richer households upon the estates of Saint-Germain-des-Pres, and takes this to mean that infanticide of girls was practiced among the poor. See her study, "L'Infanticide dans le haut Moyen Age," *Annales: Economies, Sociétés, Civilisations*, 29 (1974), 315–335. It is hard, however, to reconcile the high wergilds placed upon women, even upon female fetuses, in the laws of the Alemanni and the Salian Franks, with the conscious infanticide of girls. The high wergilds rather imply that women, even female fetuses, were valued in this society.

39. Cf. *Summa domini Henrici Hostiensis*, 219ᵛ, who argues that the groom ought not to lose more than he gained in the exchange of marriage gifts, "alias sequeretur quod pauperes non possunt uxores ducere aliqua dote data." But in fact, as the letter of Pope Nicholas I makes clear, usually in the early Middle Ages the bride gave no gift at all to the groom.

40. For further comment, see my two studies, "Life Expectancies for Women in Medieval Society" (above, n. 37) and "The Generation in Medieval History," *Viator*, 5 (1974), 347–364. It is worth noting that Tacitus in his description of

David Herlihy

marriage among the Germans (*Germania*, cap. 18 and ff.) states that the barbarian women were mature at first marriage.

41. *Leges langobardorum*, ed. Beyerle, Liutprandi leges, 129.XIII, p. 161, "Interuenientem uanissimam et superstitiosa uel cupida soasionem et peruersionem apparuit modo in his temporibus, quia inlecita nobis uel cunctis nostris iudicibus coniunctio esse paruit, quoniam adulte et iam mature aetate femine copolabant sibe puerolûs paruolûs et intra etatem legetimam. . . ."

42. Cf. *Statutum potestatis communis Pistorii anni MCCLXXXXVI*, ed. L. Zdekauer (Milan, 1888), Liber III, cap. 59, p. 120, "De puellis non nubendis . . . ante duodecimum annum sue etatis expletum."

43. *Corpus iuris canonici*, ed. Friedberg. Pars secunda: Decretales Gregorii IX, Lib. IV, Tit. 11, cap. 11, pp. 676–677.

44. *Cartolare di Giovanni Scriba*, no. 101, 25 July 1156. Guglielmo Arduino and his wife Guilia sell land, and "ego preterea W. Arduinus iuro . . . quod si vos . . . petieritis mihi . . . in eo tempore quo vobis videbitur me esse perfecte etatis, faciam de supradicta venditione vobis talem cartulam qualem vester iudex laudaverit." *Ibid.*, no. 16, suggests that age twenty-five was the normal "etas legitima" or "perfecta," as it was in Roman law.

45. *Germania*, cap. 25 (*Tacitus on Britain and Germany*, p. 121).

46. *Rotuli de dominabus et pueris et puellis de XII comitatibus (1185)*, ed. John Horace Round (Publications of the Pipe Roll Society, 35; London, 1913). In counting the offspring, orphaned boys and girls without mothers are not included.

47. *Alberti Magni ordinis fratrum praedicatorum Opera Omnia* (Monasterii Westfalorum, 1955), XII, 264: "Per accidens tamen longioris vitae est femina, tum quia minus laborant, propter quod non tantum consumuntur. . . ." For further comment, see my address, *Women in Medieval Society* (Houston, Texas: University of St. Thomas, 1971), p. 6.

48. See above, n. 46.

49. *Loc. cit.*, pp. 30–31. Alda was the wife of Willelmus Marbanc, and had four children. Emma, the widow of Hugo, aged forty, had a daughter of eighteen who was already "desponsata."

50. For evidence on age of first marriage for women, drawn from saints' lives, see my study, "The Generation in Medieval History," *Viator*, 5 (1974), 356–358.

51. In the imaginative literature, both Mark of Cornwall and Aymeri of Narbonne refused to take a wife until their vassals demanded it, even threatening to make war upon them. For these and other examples of the male reluctance to marry, see my study, "The Generation in Medieval History," n. 50, above.

52. Alain de Lille, *The Complaint of Nature*, trans. Douglas M. Moffat (Yale Studies in English, 36; New York, 1908), p. 77: "On [marriage's garments] ideal pictures told of the events of marriage, though the soot of time had almost made the images to fade." *Ibid.*, p. 55, "Moreover, the natural anvils bewail the absence of their hammers, and are seen sadly to demand them."

53. At Florence in 1427, for example, brides show at first marriage an average age of less than eighteen years, while the grooms are nearly thirty.

54. Cited in Geneviève Laribière, "Le Mariage à Toulouse au XIVe et XVe siècles," *Annales du Midi*, 79 (1967), 350. At Toulouse in the late Middle Ages, according to this study, the usual age at first marriage for women was between twelve and sixteen.

55. See n. 10 above.

56. The tendency of the aristocratic family, at least in northern France, to acquire a vertical orientation in the twelfth century with close attachment to its patrimonial lands has been noted by Georges Duby, "Structures de parenté et

noblesse dans la France du Nord aux XIe et XIIe siècles," *Hommes et structures du Moyen Age* (Paris, 1973), pp. 267–285.

57. See the observations of Henry Maine, "The Early History of the Settled Property of Married Women," *Lectures on the Early History of Institutions* (New York, 1888), pp. 306–341, especially p. 335. Concerning the Indian practice, Maine states: "There is no question that . . . the widow was made to sacrifice herself in order that her tenancy for life might be got out of the way."

58. Constitutum legis Pisane civitatis," *Statuti inediti della città di Pisa del XII al XIV secolo*, ed. F. Bonaini (Florence, 1870), II, 753: "Quia cognovimus per effectum, matres circa filios in exactione dotis et antefacti non maternum affectum sed impietatem habere sepius novercalem. . . ."

59. ". . . hoc fit perraro quippe *genus mulierum avarissimum atque tenacissimum promptius est ad accipiendum quam ad dandum.*" For the history of the phrase, see Ercole, "Vicende storiche," *AG*, 81 (1908), 93.

60. In 1579 the commune of Correggio limited bequests and donations to wives "fatte per ben pubblico e per conservazione delle famiglie et agnitioni, quali bene spesso vengono ruvinate per gli eccessive legati et donationi, che giornalmente vengono fatte alle donne, senza aver riguardo alla conservazione dell'agnatione." Cited in Brandileone, "Rapporti patrimoniali," p. 318.

II

Vices, Virtues, and Popular Preaching

Siegfried Wenzel
University of Pennsylvania

When several years ago I surveyed present scholarship on the Seven Deadly Sins,[1] I raised the question of what significance the topos really had in medieval culture and pointed out, among other things, the great practical value which the scheme held, particularly in administering the sacrament of Penance. The Seven Deadly Sins clearly provided the most widely used scheme which helped a Christian to search his conscience or a priest to examine his penitent. In this paper I want to pursue a related yet substantively distinct topic: the connection of the Seven Deadly Sins with preaching during the later Middle Ages in England.

That there was such a connection can be easily documented. First of all, official church legislation, as it was established and promulgated in the diocesan statutes of several English bishops in the thirteenth century, mentions the Seven Deadly Sins as a topic which must be regularly preached throughout all parish churches. The first English documents of this nature are the statutes for the diocese of Coventry, issued by Alexander of Stavensby between 1224 and 1237. To the twenty-nine canons of his statutes Stavensby added a treatise on the Seven Deadly Sins which begins with the injunction, "Let all parishioners on all Sundays or other feasts be told by their priests: 'There are seven criminal sins which you must flee.'" The standard seven vices are then listed and briefly explained, and in the Latin text most of them are even named in English, evidently to assure that the simple parish priests got them quite right.[2]

More important for their subsequent influence than Stavensby's injunction were the nearly contemporary statutes issued probably in 1239 by the zealous and learned bishop of Lincoln, Robert Grosseteste. They begin with the following canon:

Since there is no salvation of souls without keeping the Commandments, we exhort in the Lord and firmly enjoin that each shepherd of souls and each parish priest know the Decalogue, that is, the Ten Commandments of the Mosaic Law, and preach and expound them frequently to the people in his care. Let him also know which are the seven criminal sins and preach them likewise to the people as something to be fled. Let him, moreover, know the seven sacraments of the Church, at least in a simplified way. . . . Let in addition each of them have understanding of the faith, at least in a simplified form, as it is contained in the Creed, the major as well as the minor, and in the formula beginning "Quicumque vult," which is daily recited in the Church at Prime.[3]

Grosseteste's canon was immediately taken up by his fellow bishops all over England and reappears during the next half century in statutes for the dioceses of Worcester, Norwich, Winchester, Durham, Ely, Wells, Carlisle, York, and Exeter.[4] We notice that this statute is born of the bishop's concern about the perpetual problem of ignorant priests, a concern which can be followed in church legislation from the earliest times on. What is particularly relevant here is that in England during the 1230's the scheme of the Seven Deadly Sins became officially part of the most basic elements which a priest should know and which he was legally required to expound from the pulpit. Besides the Seven Deadly Sins such basic elements came to include the Ten Commandments, the Creed, the seven sacraments, the Lord's Prayer, the seven virtues, the works of mercy, and similar schemes. I shall refer to them henceforth simply as "catechetical matters."

Another set of constitutions confirmed this development and, in addition, made the requirement to preach such catechetical matters more specific. They are the famous Lambeth Constitutions issued by Archbishop John Pecham in 1281. Promulgated for the entire province of Canterbury, they would have been binding for the clergy of nearly all the dioceses in medieval England. Canon 9 establishes and commands that each priest who has the cure of souls, four times a year, that is, during each quarter of the year, on one or several feast days, himself or through a substitute, must expound to his people in their vernacular language, without any subtle and fanciful embellishment: the fourteen articles of faith, the ten commandments of the Decalogue, the two precepts of the gospel, that is, the twin commandments of love, further the seven works of mercy, the seven capital sins with their offspring, the seven chief virtues, and the seven sacraments of grace.[5]

This canon was very widely distributed and reappears in many pastoral handbooks up until the 1540's. In the fourteenth century it was officially incorporated in the constitutions for the province of York and translated into English, and thus became binding for the northern dioceses as well.[6]

By their very nature, legal thought and actual legislation are apt to hobble one or more decades behind the time, and medieval church law was no exception. The gist of Archbishop Pecham's constitutions had been anticipated two generations earlier by a handbook for parish priests which is now little known but throughout the thirteenth and fourteenth centuries was widely influential on similar manuals and sermons. This is the *Summa brevis* (beginning with the words, "Qui bene presunt presbiteri") compiled by Richard of Leicester *alias* Wethringsette, who was Master of Arts and Chancellor of Cambridge University by 1222.[7] Wethringsette outlines what a parish priest must know and must teach his flock:

What belongs most basically to faith and morals and must be preached very frequently are the Creed with its twelve articles of faith, the Lord's Prayer with its seven petitions, the general and particular gifts of God, especially the Seven Gifts of the Holy Ghost . . . . The four cardinal . . . and three theological virtues. And above all the seven capital vices are to be preached.[8]

The list includes some further catechetical matters, all of which are then explained and elucidated with the help of biblical and patristic quotations, commonplaces, and similes. As a peculiarly noteworthy feature, the work presents much of its doctrinal matter in verses, many of which are taken from the writings of

William de Montibus, who had taught at Mont Ste.-Geneviève in Paris and was Chancellor at Lincoln, where he directed the cathedral school, from about 1190 to 1213.[9] I single out Wethringsette's *Summa brevis* for special mention because in my view it holds an important intermediate position between similar endeavors to educate the clergy and to collect didactic material made during the twelfth century, notably among the "Paris Masters,"[10] and subsequent handbooks of like nature produced in England during the thirteenth and fourteenth centuries.[11]

Wethringsette's compilation brings us to another area in which the traditional Seven Deadly Sins were expressly recommended for regular preaching, the *Artes praedicandi*. Alanus of Lille in his *Summa de arte praedicatoria* devotes thirty-six of its forty-eight chapters to the question of what subjects a priest is to preach about, and in seven successive chapters he collects a fair amount of illustrative material for the Deadly Sins.[12] More briefly, an *Art of Preaching* perhaps written by William of Auvergne, Bishop of Paris, declares that "the vehement deprecation of the vices and the commendation of the virtues are very useful in preaching,"[13] and Humbertus de Romanis in his constitutions for the Dominican order lists "the virtues and vices" as two of the twelve subjects which Friars Preachers are to treat regularly.[14] Towards the end of the thirteenth century, the Franciscan theologian John of Wales recommends in his *Ars praedicandi*: "In the Sunday sermon it is always fitting to mention the virtues and the vices generally, in order to commend the former and to deprecate the latter."[15]

Another work by John of Wales, the *Moniloquium*, moves the Seven Deadly Sins and their opposite virtues decidedly into the front line of sermon topics. This treatise, which furnishes basic material for young preachers, begins with a reference to the Rule of St. Francis, who "admonished his brethren . . . to preach to the people the vices and virtues, punishment, and glory, in brief speech."[16] John's work accordingly elaborates the announced four topics, with the section on the vices being over four times as long as the other three together. This tetrad of *praedicabilia* became somewhat of a commonplace, so that even Wyclif, certainly no friend of the friars, used it when he chastised them: "And yet" he says, "they do not tell shortly nor plainly the Gospel, and vices and virtues and pains and joys, but make long tales of fables or chronicles or commend their own novelties."[17]

Despite Wyclif's criticism, there is clear evidence that the injunctions of diocesan statutes as well as of the *Artes praedicandi* were indeed carried out in actual preaching. Enough sermons made in the thirteenth, fourteenth, and fifteenth centuries have been preserved to show us that one or another or all of the Seven Deadly Sins and their opposite virtues were in fact expounded from the pulpit everywhere. Illustrations may be found in the studies by Owst[18] and Bloomfield.[19]

What I have presented so far is well enough known. I have rehearsed it here as an introduction to the remainder of this paper in which I want to examine a particular handbook for preachers whose contents not only provide a fine insight into subject matter and techniques of popular preaching in the fourteenth and fifteenth centuries, but have also for years attracted the interest of students of Middle English literature, particularly of the religious lyric. This is the *Fasciculus morum*,[20] so called, I suppose, because its author has collected moral matter and tied it together into a neat "bundle." The treatise, which easily fills a medium-sized quarto volume of the period (or more than five hundred double-spaced typed pages), has been preserved in twenty-eight known manuscripts, of which four are more or less abbreviated versions.[21] In addition, I have collected some twenty references to the work from book catalogues, wills, and inventories made between A.D. 1409 and the middle of the sixteenth century. If not a best-seller, it clearly was a popular book, evidently read in all parts of England, from Canterbury, London, and Winchester to Yorkshire and Durham, from Worcester in the west to Wisbech in East Anglia. At least three copies went to the Continent in the fifteenth century, to Germany, Spain, and Italy respectively, though I doubt that they had much circulation or influence there. As to its social distribution, the records of ownership clearly show the work to have been a clergyman's book. In the fifteenth century, copies existed at several colleges of the universities at Oxford and Cambridge, at what now would be called a "public school" (in the British sense) at Winchester, and in the library of a London hospital for the blind. The work is associated with masters and doctors of theology, with monks and friars, with large religious communities of men (St. Augustine's at Canterbury) and of women (Syon Monastery), and with a number of secular parish priests and chaplains. All of this agrees well with the purpose for which the book was written. The only puzzling note in this respect comes from the will of Thomas Dorchester, a merchant member of the Ironmongers' Company of London. What possible use an ironmonger may have had for a Latin tome on morals and religion I must refrain from speculating on.

Other bibliographical features remain shrouded in greater mist. Who wrote the treatise cannot be said with certainty. The manuscripts actually offer three names, all of Franciscan friars, and of the three a certain Robert Selk is the most likely candidate, even though so far no historical personage by that name has come to light. Equally hazy is the date of composition. The earliest copies can, on paleographical grounds, be assigned to the very end of the fourteenth century, and we know that copies existed in 1409 and 1412. The latest references in the text to an historical event are to the siege of Kenilworth (1266) and to King Edward I (who succeeded his father in 1272), and the latest literary references are to the *Summa confessorum* by John of Freiburg, written before 1298, and *perhaps* to a sermon by Duns Scotus, who is known to have lectured at Oxford about 1303–1304. On the other hand, Thomas Aquinas is not yet referred to as "Saint," and a reference to the shield of arms of the King of England points to a date before 1340. All things considered, then, an approximate dating in the reign of King Edward II seems most likely.[22]

I can be a little more definite about the provenance of the work. The reference to Kenilworth already alluded to involves a penitent knight who told the story of his conversion "to the brethren (or friars) of Coventry." Another story deals with two named friars of the convent of Salop (or Shrewsbury). A third story relates what a supernatural voice told an anchoress of holy life, who transmitted the message to the Bishop of Worcester. None of these tales, to my knowledge, occurs elsewhere before *Fasciculus morum* was composed, and it thus stands to reason that the treatise originated in the custody of Worcester. Even more definite is its association with the Franciscan order. Not only do those manuscripts which ascribe the treatise name a Franciscan, but the text itself contains several references to St. Francis, who is always held up as a model of outstanding virtue. But most telling is the very beginning of the book. After a rather rhetorical preface which reveals nothing of substance, the anonymous author begins:

As it is stated in the *Rule* of blessed Father Francis and decreed to the Church elsewhere, we are held to denounce and preach to the people the vices and virtues, punishment and glory, in brief words. Therefore, we shall start with the description of the vices and end with the virtues, first in general and then in particular. But since I consider seven capital vices and seven opposed virtues, this treatise is called *Fasciculus morum* and is divided into seven parts, in each of which the description of a vice will be followed, at the end, by a virtue, as the uprooter of every evil; because "that whose end is good, is in itself all good."[23]

We recognize the four subjects of preaching, given indeed in the Second Rule of St. Francis[24] and reflected, as we have seen, in John of Wales, Wyclif, and elsewhere.

True to his announced plan, after a succinct discussion of sin in general the author takes up the traditional series of the Seven Deadly Sins and pursues it from pride to lechery. Perhaps a brief comment on the order of the vices is appropriate at this point. Throughout the later Middle Ages, the most commonly encountered sequence of capital vices is that set forth by St. Gregory: pride, envy, wrath, sloth, avarice, gluttony, and lechery.[25] In St. Gregory's view, this order is based on human psychology, and the vices are linked thus because each vice rises from the preceding and leads to the following one.[26] This sequence can be, and indeed was, represented by the mnemonic word *siiaagl*, made up of the initial letters of the Latin terms for the sins. *Fasciculus morum* presents a minor variation of this standard sequence in that it places avarice before, not after, sloth. Morton Bloomfield has given some attention to the varieties one encounters in the sequence of the Seven Deadly Sins during the later Middle Ages and would explain a minor variation such as that found in *Fasciculus morum* as a confusion due to having two A's next to each other in the mnemonic word (for *avaritia* and *accidia*).[27] But there is a little more reason to it. As becomes clear in the course of the treatise, the author of *Fasciculus morum* explicitly connects the Seven Deadly Sins with the conventional Three Enemies of Man (World—Flesh—Devil), and for this reason sloth, which by 1300 had normally come to be considered a sin of the flesh,[28] had to go with gluttony and lechery and therefore follows after avarice, *the* sin of the world. I dwell on this seemingly insignificant point because, like the proverbial grain of sand that reveals the grandeur of God, the change is absolutely characteristic of the thoughtfulness and skill that have gone into the composition of the treatise.

A similar change occurs in the concomitant series of main virtues: humility, patience, love, poverty, spiritual occupation, sobriety, and chastity. These are, of course, the so-called remedial virtues, not the cardinal-plus-theological ones found elsewhere.[29] Especially noteworthy is the choice of poverty against avarice in place of the more normal virtue of mercy or generosity or almsgiving[30]—a change quite true to character in a treatise written by a follower of *il poverello*.

Each of the seven parts, then, discusses one chief vice and does so with the help of several repeated topics or considerations, such as the definition of the given vice, reasons for shunning it, comparisons of the vice which will illustrate its hideous or foolish nature, its species, and its evil effects. Next, the opposite virtue is introduced as the vice's "uprooter" (*extirpatrix*) or its fighting opponent (*pugil, athleta,* or *expugnatrix*) and similarly defined, illustrated, occasionally divided into species, and frequently elaborated by recommendations on how it may be acquired. The general rhetoric of the treatise, its mode of development, particularly for the vices, thus follows the example for this kind of literature set by the *Summa de vitiis et de virtutibus* of William Peraldus.

Into this fairly simple structure the author has inserted some other matters, such as the Decalogue, the Lord's Prayer, the articles of faith, the works of mercy, and so forth, in which we again meet the catechetical matters demanded by church legislation to be regularly expounded from the pulpit. These appear at various appropriate places and are dealt with rather briefly. Two other subjects, however, receive much more extensive treatment and consequently swell their respective sections beyond the normal proportions. In the first case,[31] the discussion of charity (which is the virtue opposed to envy) leads to the question how lost charity can be recovered. The answer is: by meditating on the passion of Christ, and a series of chapters then speak of various aspects of Christ's suffering and His cross. With this, Part III of the treatise is formally ended, yet the author continues it by expanding on "other ways in which Christ has shown His mercy" and gives a lengthy review of Christ's life from the incarnation to the sending of the Holy Spirit, and a final chapter on the Blessed Trinity. The reasons for the long expansion are not difficult to see. For one, it presents the substance of the central articles of the Creed, a catechetical matter which elsewhere in *Fasciculus morum* is treated only summarily. More important is the fact that by including the life of Christ the author has managed to incorporate a central topic of Franciscan spirituality and preaching, and to incorporate it at the most fitting point, the discussion of charity. How vital, how close to the preacher's heart the review of Christ's life was can incidentally be judged by the great number of English verses clustered in this section—a phenomenon which parallels what we find in contemporary sermons on the passion and the life of Christ, and which indeed agrees with what we know about the history of the Middle English religious lyric.[32]

My remarks on the contents and structure of *Fasciculus*

morum suggest that its author has exercised firm and intelligent control over his rich, diversified subject matter. All too often in handbooks of this nature one gets the impression that after laying out the scheme of the Seven Deadly Sins as the ground plan for his work, the author shows little further concern for the coherence and fitness of his structure. In contrast, *Fasciculus morum* resembles the great *summae* of scholastic theology by its thoughtful composition and logical integration. This structural control shows even in small matters, when for example the discussion of each vice and virtue is introduced with a *divisio* announcing the topics to be discussed, and in the subsequent development the single parts are clearly marked, usually by number and a topical word (such as, "in the second place we shall speak of X"). Another interesting feature that reveals the same control is the author's consciousness of such repetitions in his subject matter as inevitably occur. At such points he frequently abbreviates his treatment and puts in a cross reference.

Cross references suggest a reference book, and it is time now to ask how *Fasciculus morum* was intended to be used. It professes to be a preacher's aid, but it obviously does not furnish ready-made sermons to be simply read from the pulpit. It does, however, present a combination of abstract doctrinal matter with concrete images and illustrative stories which were to be used in preaching, so that one might think of it as a compendium, a thesaurus which preachers would study and from which they would cull their material. The extant manuscripts allow us, however, to understand the actual use of the book much more definitely. A number of them contain a series of forty-two sermon outlines for the Sundays and major feasts from Advent to Trinity Sunday. These are relatively short paragraphs which give a model introduction for a sermon on a given theme, lead up to the division of the theme, and then refer to specific sections in *Fasciculus morum* for the further development of the sermon divisions. To illustrate the procedure I quote the sermon for the Second Sunday after Easter. It is one of the shorter outlines but in its structure representative of them all.

"You should follow in His footsteps," I Peter 2:21. With our physical sight we observe that masons, carpenters, writers, and in brief craftsmen of almost any trade, if they want to work well and rightly and achieve the due result of their work, have need of examining and following a trustworthy model, so that by it they may be guided the better in their own labors. Now, all Christians who wish to come to eternal happiness have need of a like model. But none better can be found than the life of Christ. Hence, after the advice of blessed Peter, "You should follow in His footsteps." Concerning this we must notice that Christ, like a good leader, has gone before us on a threefold way: that of humility and obedience, for which see Part I, chap. 8; that of poverty and patience, for which see Part IV, chap. 5; and that of purity and continence, for which see Part VII. Hence for all these things we can say with Genesis 33:14: "Let my Lord pass before His servant, and I will softly follow in His footsteps."[33]

Readers familiar with medieval *artes praedicandi* or actual sermons will recognize in this outline the typical structure of a simplified "modern" or "university" sermon.[34] After stating the theme ("You should follow in His footsteps"), the outline provides an introduction to the sermon by means of a simile from everyday life: masons, carpenters, scribes, and other craftsmen need a good model; so do we if we want to come to heaven, and for that our model is the life of Christ. Then the theme is restated and immediately divided into three parts: Christ has gone the way of humility, poverty, and purity. For each part a reference is given to the book and chapter of *Fasciculus morum* which treat the respective virtue fully. After this, the outline closes with a biblical quotation which verbally contains the word or words of the sermon theme that has been divided and developed: "Let my Lord pass before His servant, and I will softly follow in His footsteps." This, too, is a device recommended by contemporary treatises on the art of preaching.[35]

These sermon outlines, therefore, lead the preacher from a given theme directly to the vices and virtues, that is, to the main subject matter of *Fasciculus morum*. They form, as it were, the key to unlock the treasures compiled in the handbook and make them quickly available to the hard-working priest who, on Saturday evening, is faced with the task of writing up a sermon for next morning. *Fasciculus morum*, incidentally, is not the only treatise that was provided with such a key. The extremely popular *Dieta salutis*, a work very similar in scope to *Fasciculus morum*, is regularly accompanied in the manuscripts by a set of sermonettes which begin with the words "Abiciamus opera tenebrarum," that is, a theme taken from the Epistle of the First Sunday in Advent.[36] I have likewise found three folios entitled "Adaptations of all the sermons contained in this book as they pertain to the Saturdays, Sundays, and feast days of the entire year," as well as to the saints' feasts, in a manuscript from St. Edmund's Abbey written about 1300.[37] The works thus keyed to sermon themes in this case are the *Summa de virtutibus* by Peraldus and a treatise on the Seven Deadly Sins derived from Peraldus.[38]

Was *Fasciculus morum* in fact ever used for its intended purpose? The number of about fifty known manuscripts, whether still extant or now lost, speaks for some degree of popularity. There is also independent evidence that in the fifteenth century *Fasciculus morum* was indeed read and used. The most interesting testimony I have come across appears in a large compilation of pious stories now preserved in the Lambeth Palace library. It was made in 1448 by William Chartham, monk of St. Augustine's monastery at Canterbury. Chartham's work begins with a longish preface which allows us a charming glimpse into the monk's character and activity. He tells us that from his childhood on he loved to read, and his coverage was wide but not indiscriminate. He stayed away from anagogical interpretations because they went over his head. Neither did he care for "the doubtful claims of philosophers" or "the empty fables of jesters," for the obvious moral reasons. Instead, Chartham says, "I eagerly attended to pious stories such as I could find in the *Lives of the Fathers*, in their *Collationes* and *Institutiones*, in the *Gesta Romanorum*, in chronicles, and in other treatises that foster the salvation of the soul and provide an example of the good life." And he continues:

As I read very many things in codices belonging to others that I borrowed, things which I could not meditate upon with enough leisure, and many other things on ragged leaves, almost destroyed by old age, which—if they had not been quickly copied—would have come to few people's knowledge, I have put together in one volume what has given me pleasure, for the praise of God and—so I hope—for the delight and benefit of many young people. . . . Since [this book] furnishes its readers not solid food but, as it were, milk for little children, let it be called *Speculum parvulorum.*[39]

Although Chartham does not actually name *Fasciculus morum* among his sources, he copied more than twenty pious tales from it verbatim. The stories appear at different spots in the collection and always in larger blocks, so that one gains the impression that once Chartham's attention was caught by a tale, he could hardly refrain from copying the next one, too, and then the one thereafter as well. His preface, incidentally, speaking of tattered old codices that were falling apart or becoming otherwise illegible, may help to explain the long gap in time between the supposed date of composition of *Fasciculus morum* (about 1320) and the date of the oldest surviving copies (about 1400). Very probably, like Chartham's sources, the first generation of copies of *Fasciculus morum* was simply read to shreds.

Chartham's interest in *Fasciculus morum* was not an isolated phenomenon, and similar miscellanies can be cited whose compilers excerpted passages from our handbook with or without acknowledgment. The same holds true for the appearance of material from *Fasciculus morum* in actual sermons. In leafing through fourteenth- or fifteenth-century manuscripts, again and again one runs across a passage or entire sermon that closely resembles a chapter from the handbook without naming it. But at least one sermon collection quotes *Fasciculus morum* by name. This is a series of English sermons preserved in several fifteenth-century manuscripts and partially related to John Mirk's *Festial.*[40] Here a Christmas sermon tells a story about two envious neighbors who are seen in hell tearing each other to pieces. The tale is introduced with "I find in *Fasciculus morum*, Part II, chapter 7, that once upon a time there were two neighbors."[41] A similar phrase introduces another tale from the handbook in a different sermon,[42] and elsewhere in the collection appear other tales without such identification. Nor has the anonymous compiler used *Fasciculus morum* only for illustrative material, but on at least one occasion (the writing of his sermon for Ash Wednesday) he has borrowed, with the material, the structure of an entire chapter. In this case a marginal reference to *Fasciculus morum* leaves no doubt about his indebtedness.[43]

The purpose of our handbook and its actual use by preachers are also reflected in its style and texture, and we must now take a closer look at the material which fills the seven parts on the Deadly Sins. I quote in illustration a short paragraph from the part on pride, which is quite representative of what one finds throughout the handbook. Under the topic "Whence pride proceeds," the author discusses pride of heart, mouth, and deed. Pride of mouth has three species, whose last—evil speech or *maliloquium*—is developed as follows:

In the third place, we must beware of evil speech, for according to the Apostle in I Cor. 15, "Evil talks corrupt good manners." For a small quantity of leaven corrupts the entire mass of dough, and a single drop of poison can affect many once it has spread. According to St. Anselm, the tongue must be guarded most strongly, for through it all evils are suggested and carried out. And to show that it must be guarded well, it has been set, as it were, in a prison, with a wall of teeth in front of it, and lips as ramparts. In Ephesians 4 it is said, "Let no evil speech proceed out of your mouth." Whence it is well said in English,

> See and hear and hold thee still
> If thou wilt live and have thy will.

Hence we read about a holy father who saw angels rejoicing whenever the conversation was about God, but raising stained and dirty hands to their mouths when the conversation was about worldly things. When he learned this, he carried a stone in his mouth for three years, so that he might learn silence.[44]

In a single paragraph the warning against evil speech is sustained by two biblical quotations, one quotation attributed to a Doctor of the Church, three similitudes (leaven, poison, and prison walls), a proverbial verse in English, and an *exemplum* which conflates two separate stories from the *Vitae Patrum*.[45] These are all, of course, standard devices which contemporary *artes praedicandi* recommended as means of developing a sermon, and which preachers in the fourteenth and fifteenth centuries in fact relied upon constantly. Their function is to prove, to illustrate, or to strengthen the emotional impact of the specific points of faith and morals that are discussed.

What catches the reader's eye immediately are the similes and *exempla*, which stand out by their sheer bulk and number as the major pulpit devices gathered in the handbook. Similes are taken from a surprisingly wide range of life and letters. There is the field of "natural science" with the properties of stones, plants, and animals culled from the pages of learned books or encyclopedias and represented by such old favorites as the goat that grows sterile when it licks an olive, or the female stork who manages to keep her extramarital affairs hidden by taking a bath. On the other hand, many nature images come from actual observation or daily experience, such as the dancing bear that is dragged through the villages and bitten by dogs, or the difference between a hen and a falcon, which—while being respectively a common and a noble bird during their lifetime—find their status reversed in death, when the hen graces a king's table while the falcon lands on the dunghill.

Most similes, however, derive from the world of man and are linked to the main social classes. Kings and castles figure in many of them, while town life and burghers are more sparsely represented. Somewhat surprisingly, the world of the clergy furnishes hardly any images at all, though professional groups like teachers, scribes, physicians, and astronomers appear here and there. On the other hand, the common folk provide a host of similes, from the blacksmith who, with his bellows, hammer, and anvil, becomes a figure of the devil, or who plays a painful trick on unwary citizens by putting a piping-hot horseshoe in the street for them to pick up, to the tinker who wanders from village to village in search of broken pots and pans rather than beautiful bowls of gold and silver. Such interest in the lower classes extends even to their lowest members: thieves, beggars, and jugglers, who appear in a good many comparisons. One type of juggler, for instance, "kills his horse, skins it, and pretends it is dead, and then lets it come to life again"[46]—a reference perhaps to a mummers' play and here illustrative of a particular hell pain. Two other pastimes are alluded to in similar fashion. One is a puzzling game whose participants "think they are in, yet in the end they are out."[47] The other is a *ludus puellarum* played in summertime, when a poor girl is chosen to be queen and properly dressed up in the clothes of the other girls. "Looking about her in such dignity she forgets her former state and believes she really is a queen and so despises her companions. But when evening comes, each girl gets her own clothes back, and she who has seemed to be a queen, is now left poor and naked. Thus do worldlings glory in their power and rank. . . ."[48]

Games lead us to another segment of life from which many comparisons have been taken—that of children, nurses, and mothers. Some children play with tops which, in order to spin, must be whipped well. Others play with mudcakes and watermills or chase pretty butterflies which, once they are caught, turn into an ugly mess—both very fitting images indeed for the ultimate uselessness of much worldly activity. Mothers lovingly care for their children, feed them, wipe off their tears, and soothe them when they are angry. Yet they also chastise them when they get too close to fire or water. Not all children return such love. A crazy child grows the merrier, the more his mother grieves for him. More charming is the philological observation that children often confuse the consonants *r* and *l* in their pronunciation; like them, miserly grownups prefer to co*l*lect rather than co*r*rect themselves. In contrast, a child is quite willing to exchange his gold ring for an apple, and a good boy will himself take the rod to his father when he has done some wrong. Yet this world of children is not all sweetness and light. Babies cry when they are fed, even though the food is good for them; boys catch birds and pull their feathers or blind them in sport; others steal fruit from an orchard and are flogged by the gatekeeper. And sometimes, when a boy who has an apple falls into a ditch and calls for help, his playmate pretends to help him, but grabs the apple and with a laugh lets his fellow fall back. "Thus do misers in their search for worldly goods associate . . . : but when one through death falls into the pit, 'strangers spoil his labors.' "[49]

Turning from similes to illustrative stories or *exempla*, we find a similarly wide range of tales that reach from classical myth and history to events of the author's own day, from the ancient Mediterranean world to fourteenth-century England. Little needs to be said about the appearance of biblical stories that illustrate a lesson or are said to prefigure a moral point. Truly astonishing, however, is the large proportion of stories from the world of classical myth, fable, and history that have found their way into *Fasciculus morum*. There are the myths of Prometheus, Antaeus, the Gorgon, and the two tuns at the threshold of Jupiter's palace; there are Hero and Leander, Phyllis and Demophon, Atalanta and the golden apples, Acontius, and an unnamed Narcissus, from the world of classical fable; and from Troy there are stories about Helena, Cassandra, Achilles, and Ulysses. Ancient Greece furnishes tales about two handfuls of philosophers, and Greek history provides the examples of Leonidas and other military leaders, the tyrant Dionysius, and a dozen tales of Alexander the Great. Their counterparts from Roman history are even more numerous, ranging in time from the Consul Curius through the Punic and Civil Wars to the Emperor Titus.

In contrast, the world of early Christianity appears less often. Christ's coming is announced by the Sibyl, and various legends of His childhood are retold. Most stories in this group, however, concern the life of the desert fathers and are taken from the *Vitae Patrum*, which together with St. Gregory's *Dialogues* is certainly the largest contributor to this category.

But clearly the greatest number of tales derive from that vast amount of story material which originated in twelfth- and early thirteenth-century collections of *exempla* and spread from there to numerous handbooks and sermons. Many of these tell of frightful dreams and visions, of violent deaths, gruesome hell pains, and corpses on which toads and snakes feed. But a gentler note is not totally lacking. Two stories, for instance, deal with the motif of golden letters found inscribed on a man's heart because of his great love of Christ. Knights can be forgiving and generous, and friendship lasts beyond the grave. Even the glimmer of a joke appears here and there. Three companions, for example, are invited to a banquet in winter. When they are served partially spoiled fruit for dessert, one throws it away in disgust, the other gobbles it all up in his gluttony, while only the third knows how to deal with it "in courtly fashion."[50] Better known is the story of the vicar who is reproached by his bishop for giving his donkey a Christian burial; but when the bishop learns that the donkey left him forty *solidi* in its will, he quickly says, "Requiescat in pace!"[51] Similar verbal readiness is shown by the housewife who does not want to waste much cloth on her husband's shroud, and when she is reproached for this by her dying man, retorts that he has a long way ahead of him and will not want to get his hems wet.[52] Knights, too, can have fun in the exercise of chivalry. Two of them make a pact to exchange winnings at a tournament; when one, who is a coward and has achieved nothing, asks for his share of the horses that his braver companion has gained, he is very courteously given the horses —together with his share of beatings.[53] And finally, even the fabliau of the weeping bitch, so well known from the Middle English poem "Dame Sirith," appears in our handbook, where it illustrates the evil tricks of go-betweens.[54]

Time forbids dwelling on the ten or so contemporary tales, many of which refer to English cities (such as London, Norwich, Coventry, Worcester, and Shrewsbury), include a phrase or a couplet in English, and are rarely if at all found outside *Fasciculus morum*. None of them is told for its own sake. Like all the other tales and similes, they illustrate a moral point, either by exemplifying a moral stated beforehand in the text, or by being subjected to a piece-by-piece allegorization after they have been told. Both techniques are common in *Fasciculus morum*, as they are in other sermon literature. It is worth pointing out that in addition to this exemplifying function, occasionally such moralized tales or similes appear to be used in the text for a structural purpose as well and provide the frame for an entire chapter. Such a structuring function is likewise shown by two other devices often found in medieval sermons. The first is a method of amplification by which, in the words of one *Ars praedicandi*, "some preachers take the individual letters of a word and then find other words that begin with these letters."[55] The new words are then further developed. In our handbook the technique is used at least once. To illustrate the idea that pride can be overcome best by thinking of one's death, the author takes the Latin word for death, *mors*, and finds for its four letters new words which indicate four properties of death. These are: *mirum speculum* (mirror), *orologium* (clock), *raptor* (thief), and *citator* (summoner), each of which is expanded separately.[56]

The other device that has a similar structuring function is the moralized "picture." An abstract idea is visualized as a painting or statue of a person with various attributes which are then allegorized one by one and thus gradually unfold the qualities contained in the concept. For example, Prayer is depicted as a beautiful youth with a body of fire, his head raised to heaven, leaning on a long and straight lance, supported by four angels that bear scrolls with inscriptions in verse. Each of these details as well as the verses are then developed at some length and thus structure the entire discussion of the usefulness of prayer.[57] Other concepts illustrated in this fashion are Death, Flattery, the World, Justice, Love, and Gluttony. The technique has received some attention from art historians and, recently, from Beryl Smalley in her book on *English Friars and Antiquity in the Early Fourteenth Century*.[58] The occurrence of such pictures, together with the interest in classical fable and history that we noticed earlier, would justify us in ranking the author of *Fasciculus morum* with such classicizing friars as Ridewall and Holkot.

I have left for last another preaching device for which *Fasciculus morum* is justly famous, its Middle English verses.[59] There are over fifty short poems scattered through the text, ranging in length from two to fourteen lines. They are of the kind that is usually referred to as "preachers' tags," to be used at appropriate moments in a sermon in order to drive home a point or to sum up a lesson in a form that can be easily memorized. While this description is adequate enough, the label "preachers' tags" carries with it—at least to my mind—implications of non-essential triviality, which may need some revision. Here the verses not only have a variety of functions in their context, but many of them, far from being merely tacked on and hence dispensable, form an integral and necessary part of the text. Some of these verses are metrical proverbs and illustrate a moral point in much the same way as do biblical or patristic authorities. A good example is the already quoted

> See and hear and hold thee still
> If thou wilt live and have thy will,[60]

to which I shall return in a moment; or the even simpler

> Whoso will not when he may,
> He shall not when he would.[61]

These and other verses have much in common with the "Proverbs of Hending" (which, incidentally, are quoted several times in the text) and similar proverb collections.

Slightly different in function are verses that summarize material, whether it is some doctrinal matter, such as the Ten Commandments,[62] or a longer story. Foolish trust in the world, for instance, is illustrated by a tale of a juggler named Ulfrid who receives a magic, gift-producing cloak with the warning that it will lose its power as soon as its wearer grows proud. This is of course precisely what happens to poor Ulfrid, and the plot of the tale is summed up with

> The mantle which the king to Ulfrid lent,
> With hap it came, with hap it went.[63]

In this case the verses are indeed tacked on, and the story proper does not need them. In other cases, however, verses form an integral part of the tale, as in the story about an anchoress of holy life who, having for some time observed a tavern-haunting, negligent priest who mumbled and shortened his prayers, grew so worried that she asked God to reveal to her whether this man's service pleased Him at all. The answer, as one might expect, is negative, but to one's surprise the Almighty speaks it in verse and in Middle English.[64] Without these lines, the story would have no point; far from being a tag, they are its very climax.

The last mentioned case elucidates why these lines and a good number of others may be called "message verses,"[65] in which a character within a tale formulates in meter and rhyme whatever needs to be driven home with particular force. The speaker may be a divine voice heard by an anchoress, or it may be a damned soul wailing

> Alas, alas, that I was born,
> Both life and soul I am forlorn![66]

The lines I have quoted earlier, "See and hear and hold thee still," etc., actually are message verses, too, for they are spoken, or rather crowed, by the prudent rooster in the popular tale of the Three Cocks.[67] Other messages appear as inscriptions on statues or tombs, and while many are short and similar in character to such modern counterparts as "Winston tastes good, like a cigarette should," others attain considerable lyric depth and resonance, as when Christ speaks from the Cross or knocks at the gate of His beloved.

A number of these verses preserve age-old vernacular proverbs or oft-quoted sayings, but the large majority are direct translations of one or two Latin hexameters.[68] We must realize how deeply the use of such vernacular verses in preaching was indebted to similar Latin verses found in thirteenth-century and later sermon collections and handbooks. It is a curious fact that, while a large number of Middle English verses and religious lyrics are preserved in Latin handbooks (such as *Fasciculus morum*), in Latin sermons (such as the collection made by Bishop John Sheppey[69]), and in Latin commonplace books (such as Friar John Grimestone's[70]), the Middle English sermon collections produced in the fifteenth century almost completely lack vernacular verses. John Mirk's *Festial* and the Middle English sermons I referred to earlier contain hardly any verses at all; certain "messages" which in the tradition of Latin sermon manuscripts were consistently favored with a vernacular verse are here expressed in blunt prose.[71] I do not know whether this means that the fifteenth century was a more prosaic age; but it does mean that earlier preachers, in Latin and in the vernacular, took much delight in sprinkling, or peppering, their prose sermons with verses. They not only recognized the mnemonic and rhetorical or persuasive usefulness of such verse items for their audience, but must have themselves experienced genuine pleasure in turning out a good verse. There are enough instances of wit, of verbal punning, of clever linguistic skill at work in these otherwise modest verses to make me think that intelligent preachers may have had some fun with them.

These are some of the reasons why a professor of Middle English literature would spend much of his time on a Latin handbook for preachers. *Fasciculus morum* is an important document for students of fourteenth-century letters. It does not tell us much about contemporary *mores* or current social and economical problems, nor does it reflect the great concerns with philosophy, political theory, or religious controversy which exercised the minds of clerics and laymen and soon were to break up the relative unity of medieval civilization. But it does reveal what fourteenth-century Englishmen were most likely to hear from their pulpits, the topics that lay at the center of their faith, their ethics, their devotion. This importance *Fasciculus morum* shares with contemporary sermons and with such preachers' aids as Bromyard's encyclopedia, Grimestone's commonplace book, the *Gesta Romanorum*, and similar compilations. But it surpasses them by the intelligence and care with which it was written. All in all, it is a much more readable book.

It also shows us how the vices were denounced and the virtues commended during the last two medieval centuries. By 1500—and, many of us would add, already by the time Chaucer wrote the *Canterbury Tales*—that topic with its innumerable proof texts and illustrative stories had been heard so many times that it would no longer stir an audience to contrition, but lull them into a peaceful doze. Yet we must not overlook that at an earlier moment in the history of Western Europe the topic and the subject matter I have pursued had been fresh. At that earlier time men of intelligence and learning cast their nets widely for new material which they could use in preaching to the people, material such as then passed as scientific lore, or classical myths and fables, or powerful tales from the Far East, or moralized pictures visualizing abstract concepts, together with stories and similes from their audience's own experience, including even popular games and songs. That toward the end of the Middle Ages this material had grown rather stale should not blind us to the fact that *Fasciculus morum* belongs to an exciting endeavor to reach out for new subject matter from hitherto untapped sources and areas. When Friar Robert Selk, or whoever it was, wrote his book, the sticks he gathered into his bundle were still fresh enough to strike home a lesson with force, and solid enough to light a good warming fire in the hearts of his audience.

Notes

1. S. Wenzel, "The Seven Deadly Sins: Some Problems of Research," *Speculum*, 43 (1968), 1–22, esp. 12 ff.
2. *Councils and Synods*, ed. F. M. Powicke and C. R. Cheney, vol. II.i (Oxford, 1964), p. 214. The translations are my own.
3. *Ibid.*, II.i, p. 268.
4. *Ibid.*, II.i, pp. 304, 345, 403, 423, 516, 609 f., 628, 659, and II.ii, p. 1017.
5. *Ibid.*, II.ii, pp. 901–902.
6. Cf. D. L. Douie, *Archbishop Pecham* (Oxford, 1952), pp. 138–142; *Councils and Synods*, vol. II.ii, p. 888 and n. 3.
7. On Wethringsette see A. B. Emden, *A Biographical Register of the University of Cambridge to 1500* (Cambridge, 1963), pp. 367 and 679, with further literature. See also footnote 9, below. Fifty-seven manuscripts of the *Summa brevis* are listed in the unpublished D. Phil. thesis of Father Leonard E. Boyle, "A Study of the Works Attributed to William of Pagula" (Oxford, 1956), II, 20–22.
8. British Museum, MS Royal 4.B.viii, fol. 222ʳ.
9. See H. Mackinnon, "William de Montibus, a Medieval Teacher," in *Essays in Medieval History Presented to Bertie Wilkinson*, ed. T. A. Sandquist and M. R. Powicke (Toronto, 1969), pp. 32–45.
10. See J. W. Baldwin, *Masters, Princes, and Merchants: The Social Views of Peter the Chanter and His Circle* (Princeton, 1970).
11. Such literature has been frequently surveyed. See, for example, E. J. Arnould, *Le "Manuel des péchés": Étude de littérature religieuse anglo-normande* (Paris, 1940), pp. 1–59; W. A. Pantin, *The English Church in the Fourteenth Century* (Cambridge, 1955), chapters ix–x; and the work by L. E. Boyle, cited in note 7, above.
12. Chapters 4–10; *Patrologia latina*, CCX, 119–133.
13. A. de Poorter, "Un Manuel de prédication médiévale. Le MS. 97 de Bruges," *Revue Néo-scolastique*, 25 (1923), 199.
14. *Liber de instructione officialium ordinis fratrum praedicatorum*; quoted by D. Roth, *Die mittelalterliche Predigttheorie und das Manuale curatorum des Johann Ulrich Surgant*, "Basler Beiträge zur Geschichtswissenschaft," 58 (Basel and Stuttgart, 1956), p. 56.
15. Bodleian Library, MS 571, fol. 169ʳ.
16. Peterhouse (Cambridge), MS 200, fol. 1ʳ.
17. F. D. Matthew, ed., *The English Works of Wyclif, Hitherto Unprinted*. EETS, 74 (London, 1880), p. 50. For other passages, see H. G. Pfander, *The Popular Sermon of the Medieval Friar in England* (New York, 1937), p. 11.
18. G. R. Owst, *Preaching in Medieval England* (Cambridge, 1926) and *Literature and Pulpit in Medieval England* (Cambridge, 1933; rev. ed., Oxford, 1961), *passim*.
19. M. W. Bloomfield, *The Seven Deadly Sins* (East Lansing, 1952), pp. 160 ff. and 209 ff.
20. Previously described by A. G. Little in *Studies in English Franciscan History* (Manchester, 1917), pp. 139–157. Professor Frances A. Foster worked for many years toward an edition of the treatise. Her materials, deposited at the Beinecke Library at Yale, have been temporarily placed in the library of the University of North Carolina at Chapel Hill for my use. I have examined all manuscripts in England and Scotland *in situ*, thanks to a Guggenheim fellowship.
21. A more detailed analysis of the manuscripts and related questions will appear with full documentation in a forthcoming book on *Fasciculus morum*, which is to contain a critical edition of the English verses.

22. See further Little, *Studies*, pp. 142–145; and F. A. Foster, "Some English Words from the *Fasciculus Morum*," in *Essays and Studies in Honor of Carleton Brown* (New York, 1940), p. 149. This date also agrees with inferences drawn from a comparative study of several *exempla*.

23. Bodleian Library, MS Rawlinson C. 670, fol. 7ʳ. All quotations of *Fasciculus morum* are taken from this manuscript, and translations are my own.

24. *Regula II*, cap. 9; *Opuscula sancti Patris Francisci Assisinensis*, "Bibliotheca Franciscana ascetica medii aevi," I (Quaracchi, 1904), 71.

25. Cf. Bloomfield, *The Seven Deadly Sins*, p. 72 and *passim*.

26. For various schemes of rationalizing the number and order of the capital vices, see S. Wenzel, *The Sin of Sloth: Acedia in Medieval Thought and Literature* (Chapel Hill, 1967), pp. 38–46; and "The Seven Deadly Sins . . . ," *Speculum*, 43 (1968), 3–12.

27. Bloomfield, *The Seven Deadly Sins*, pp. 88, 105–106.

28. Cf. S. Wenzel, *The Sin of Sloth*, pp. 164–168; and "The Three Enemies of Man," *Mediaeval Studies*, 29 (1967), 47–66.

29. For example, in the *Summa de virtutibus* by William Peraldus.

30. Avarice is opposed by mercy in the treatise "Postquam dictum est"; see S. Wenzel, "The Source for the *Remedia* of the Parson's Tale," *Traditio*, 27 (1971), 433–453. *Largitas* is the remedial virtue, for example, in John of Wales, *Moniloquium*, MS Peterhouse 200, fol. 55ʳ.

31. The other expansion occurs in Part V, where the virtue opposed to sloth, spiritual activity, leads to a long discussion of (*a*) Penance, with its three parts of contrition, confession, and satisfaction; and (*b*) man's battle against the Three Enemies, which in turn are related to the theological and cardinal virtues.

32. R. H. Robbins, "The Authors of the Middle English Religious Lyrics," *JEGP*, 39 (1940), 230–238; R. Woolf, *The English Religious Lyric in the Middle Ages* (Oxford, 1968), Chapter 2; D. Gray, *Themes and Images in the Medieval English Religious Lyric* (London, 1972), Chapter 7.

33. Bodleian Library, MS 187, fol. 216ᵛ.

34. For detailed discussions of the structure of later medieval sermons, see Th.-M. Charland, *Artes praedicandi: Contribution à l'histoire de la rhétorique au moyen âge* (Paris, 1936); W. O. Ross, *Middle English Sermons*, EETS, 209 (London, 1940), pp. xliii–lv; and James J. Murphy, *Rhetoric in the Middle Ages: A History of Rhetorical Theory from St. Augustine to the Renaissance* (Berkeley, 1974).

35. Robert of Basevorn, for example, calls this figure *unitio*; see his *Forma praedicandi*, ed. Charland, *Artes praedicandi*, p. 306.

36. Extant in many manuscripts, and often printed with *Dieta salutis* as attributed to Bonaventura (for example, Bergamo: Petrus de Quarengiis, 1497–1498; Paris: Pierre le Dru, *ca.* 1495).

37. British Museum, MS Royal 11.B.iii, fol. 278ʳ–280ᵛ.

38. This is the anonymous treatise "Primo videndum est," for which see S. Wenzel, "The Source of Chaucer's Seven Deadly Sins," *Traditio*, 30 (1974), 351–378.

39. Lambeth Palace, MS 78, fol. 1ʳ⁻ᵛ. See also M. R. James and C. Jenkins, *A Descriptive Catalogue of the Manuscripts in the Library of Lambeth Palace* (Cambridge, 1930–1932), p. 129.

40. British Museum, MSS Royal 18.B.xxv and Harley 2247. See L. L. Steckman, "A Late Fifteenth-Century Revision of Mirk's *Festial*," *SP*, 34 (1937), 36–48; D. S. Brewer, "Observations on a Fifteenth-Century Manuscript," *Anglia*, 72 (1954), 390–399. The sermons have been recently edited by Mrs. Susan Powell in a Uni-

versity of London Ph.D. thesis. John Mirk's *Festial* is edited in EETS, e.s., 96; it lacks the material from *Fasciculus morum*.

41. MS Harley 2247, fol. 7^r; Royal 18.B.xxv, fol. 19^v.

42. MS Harley 2247, fol. 70^v; Royal 18.B.xxv, fol. 46^r.

43. "Nota de Confessione. Hec fasciculus morum parte 5^a capitulo 11." MS Harley 2247, fol. 49^v; the Royal MS lacks the note.

44. Bodleian Library, MS Rawlinson, C. 670, fol. 10^{r-v}.

45. *Vitae patrum*, III, 36, and V, 7; *Patrologia latina*, LXXIII, 762 and 865. Cf. F. C. Tubach, *Index exemplorum*, "FF Communications," 204 (Helsinki, 1969), Nos. 245 and 4627.

46. MS Rawlinson C.670, fol. 23^v.

47. *Ibid.*, fol. 81^r. The game is elsewhere called *botecoraye*; see G. R. Owst, *Notes and Queries*, 152 (1927), 244.

48. *Ibid.*, fol. 11^v.

49. *Ibid.*, fol. 81^r.

50. *Ibid.*, fol. 40^r; cf. Tubach, *Index exemplorum*, No. 318.

51. *Ibid.*, fol. 69^r; cf. Tubach, No. 376.

52. *Ibid.*, fol. 114^r; cf. Tubach, No. 4356.

53. *Ibid.*, fol. 90^v; cf. Tubach, No. 2965.

54. *Ibid.*, fol. 138^r; cf. Tubach, No. 661.

55. Thomas Waleys, *De modo componendi sermones*, ed. Charland, *Artes praedicandi*, p. 396.

56. MS Rawlinson C.670, fol. 21^r.

57. *Ibid.*, fol. 110^v. This "picture" also appears in Holkot's *Moralitates*, the miscellany contained in MS Harley 7322, and the *Gesta Romanorum*.

58. B. Smalley, *English Friars* . . . (Oxford, 1960), pp. 165 ff., and *passim*.

59. They have been commented upon by R. H. Robbins, ed., *Secular Lyrics of the XIVth and XVth Centuries* (2nd ed.; Oxford, 1955), pp. xviii–xix (and more fully in his University of Cambridge dissertation, "The Medieval English Religious Lyric," 1937); R. Woolf, *The English Religious Lyric in the Middle Ages*, *passim*; David L. Jeffrey, *The Early English Lyric and Franciscan Spirituality* (Lincoln, Neb., 1975); and elsewhere. I am currently preparing a full critical edition of these verses.

60. Cf. C. Brown and R. H. Robbins, *The Index of Middle English Verse* (New York, 1943), No. 3081.

61. *Ibid.*, No. 4151; see also B. J. and H. W. Whiting, *Proverbs, Sentences, and Proverbial Phrases from English Writings Mainly Before 1500* (Cambridge, Mass., 1968), W275.

62. Brown and Robbins, *Index*, No. 3254.

63. *Ibid.*, No. 3287.

64. *Ibid.*, No. 1935.

65. I have used this term in "The English Verses in the *Fasciculus morum*," in *Chaucer and Middle English Studies in Honour of Rossell Hope Robbins*, ed. Beryl Rowland (London, 1974), pp. 230–254.

66. Brown and Robbins, *Index*, No. 142B.

67. Tubach, *Index exemplorum*, No. 1134.

68. I have analyzed the precise relationships between the English verses of *Fasciculus morum* and their Latin context in the article mentioned in note 65.

69. Contained in Merton College (Oxford), MS 248. See C. Brown, *Religious Lyrics of the XIVth Century* (2nd ed., rev. G. V. Smithers; Oxford, 1952), p. xv; and G. Mifsud, "John Sheppey, Bishop of Rochester, as Preacher and Collector of Sermons," B.Litt. thesis, Oxford, 1953.

70. Cf. E. Wilson, *A Descriptive Index of the English Lyrics in John of Grime-stone's Preaching Book,* "Medium Aevum Monographs," New Series, II (Oxford, 1973).

71. For example, the fifteenth-century Middle English sermons edited by D. M. Grisdale (*Three Middle English Sermons from the Worcester Chapter Manuscript F.10,* Leeds School of English Language, Texts and Monographs, V [Leeds, 1939]) contain a scene where Christ, speaking from the cross, displays His wounds ("Bihold . . . ," p. 47) and a translation of Ecclesiasticus 7:40, "Memorare novissima" (p. 64). Both "messages" are given in verse in *Fasciculus morum* (Brown and Robbins, *Index,* Nos. 495 and 1127) and elsewhere, but are here presented in prose.

III

The Popular Dimension of the Reformation: An Essay in Methodology and Historiography

Hans J. Hillerbrand
The Graduate School and University Center
of the City University of New York

My topic is very much "in," seemingly crucial for the understanding of the Reformation, and basically insoluble.

If in my very first sentence I have not only expressed shocking skepticism but also conveyed what is customarily reserved for the last (or is not revealed at all), I hasten to emphasize that I shall be as much concerned about the various considerations along the way as the final destination. In other words, I am suggesting that the topic raises a number of methodological problems, the proper resolution of which would shed a great deal of light, I believe, on the way we ought to understand the Reformation.

The topic is "in." In recent years historical scholarship has become fascinated by the exploration of new ways of examining and explaining the past, and in so doing it has moved away, however slightly, from the customary predilection for institutional or intellectual history. Reformation historians ought to be particularly receptive to such new approaches in that the use of traditional ways and methods of research in their area of specialization—no matter how successful—may be said to have reached a point of diminishing returns, if not a state of exhaustion. The embarrassingly large number of monographs on the still-unresolved question of Luther's so-called "evangelical discovery" pointedly testifies to this state of affairs, though one might observe that as long as such pursuit gives pleasure to its practitioners without harming others, the state of affairs is surely tolerable.[1]

I emphasize the stagnation of Reformation research in view of the fact that for the past two generations Reformation scholars have been preoccupied with the study and delineation of "ideal types" of ideas and events—the study of organizational structures, and, more extensively, the study of formal theological systems. While the results have been, by and large, impressive, this approach, on account of its restrictive propensity, has run the danger of losing touch with historical reality. Our knowledge is uneven. We know far better what the formal structures were than how they worked in actual practice, far better what the norms of belief were than what was actually believed.[2] This failure to distinguish between the "ideal" and the "real" has been particularly discomforting and misleading when comparisons were made—between the religiosity of the late Middle Ages and the Reformation, for example, or between the mainstream Reformation and its radical fringe—for frequently the shift from one to the other has also entailed a shift in methodology. Quite a few of the unresolved issues in Reformation research surely must be traced to this uncertainty.

Secondly, the topic may be said to be tied to the question of the very essence of the Reformation itself. The matter is complicated, but, since the Reformation was a coat of many colors, a variety of definitions and perspectives are possible. I presume that most will agree, moreover, that the Reformation was more than the sum total of the reflections of theologians, that it was, rather, a phenomenon affecting European society at large. If this was so, we deprive ourselves of understanding it unless we see its popular dimension clearly. We may say only little about the impact of the Reformation upon society unless we know something about the number of its partisans. We may remain ignorant of the actual meaning of the Reformation in a given locale—whether it was from "above" or from "below," to use phrases that have become popular—unless we have a notion as to the quantitative dimension of the movement which precipitated the change.[3] Again, it is futile to talk about the loss of popular support of the Reformation as a result of the German Peasants'

War—as one of the orthodoxies of Reformation historiography has it—unless we have a clear notion as to the size of that support prior to 1524.[4]

Of course I am carrying coals to Newcastle. The two major historiographical strands of Reformation scholarship have emphasized that a significant popular dimension existed.[5] The ecclesiastical approach, on the one hand, has made the widespread popular appeal of Luther and his reforming comrades-in-arms one of its fundamental assertions. It has argued from the incisiveness of the reformers' theological position to the inevitability of a popular appeal, and thereby has vindicated the authenticity of the theology by the actual course of events. Ecclesiastically oriented Reformation scholarship, certainly of the Protestant variety, leaves little doubt that the movement possessed significant popular appeal.

The other major strand of Reformation scholarship is the Marxist one. It sees the Reformation as the ideology of the "early bourgeoisie." The Reformation, thus, was a significant, broadly based, popular movement, which, intimately related to the German Peasants' War of 1524–1525, was concerned about the comprehensive repudiation of the feudal system.[6] In short, Marxist historians accept the popular dimension of the Reformation as one of its fundamental characteristics.

The eminent differences between the two perspectives lie in the conceptual realm. While ecclesiastical historians affirm the authenticity of religious beliefs, Marxists insist that the religious phenomenon must be seen as an "ideology." There is little difference in the respective descriptive assessments of the sixteenth century, even though Marxist historiography stresses the dramatic discontinuity of the popular appeal precipitated by the German Peasants' War.

In other words, Reformation historians have employed terms that imply a significant quantitative dimension of the Reformation.[7] They have spoken of a movement, of popular support, of Luther's widespread appeal, of declining Catholic loyalty. A perusal of the introductions to the Reformation—candor compels me to include my own—shows that there has been no dearth of the use of such categories.[8] The standard shorthand version is that there was a Reformation "movement," though the exact quantitative dimension of that movement is left unsettled.[9]

The assumption of a widespread popular interest in the new religious movement requires one of two presuppositions. The first and most obvious one is to allow for the fundamentally religious character of the movement and then to inquire about the extent to which the early sixteenth century was interested in religious matters. The assumption is that religion was central to society, that people widely yearned for authentic religious exercise and experience.

Such a view tends to overlook a great deal of evidence. We surely must constantly remind ourselves that life in the early sixteenth century was burdened by long and tedious work, by omnipresent and dreadful disease. Pain and violence were no less constant companions than were poverty and illiteracy. It may well be that such a dreary life evoked the yearning for a better one, for liberation from personal bondage. Yet a life lived on the boundary of personal extinction and physical deprivation relates only with ambivalence to religious concerns.

Moreover, if we consider the widely prevailing theological illiteracy in the early sixteenth century, it becomes obvious that most people were ill-equipped to perceive and understand even the very outlines of the Christian affirmation. Such basics of the Christian faith as the Ten Commandments or the Lord's Prayer were deep enigmas, even as the liturgical and sacramental splendor of the church was subjected to gross and blatant misinterpretation.[10] There should be little doubt that in the early sixteenth century religion was lively, but in a special way. The visitation records, both before *and* after the Reformation, indicate that even rigid governmental mandates—not to speak of the threat of eternal damnation—could not bring the mass of people to church in a fashion becoming their souls' salvation and the tranquillity of the body politic.

I do not mean to propound a warm-up of the old Protestant

clichés of theological perversion and spiritual listlessness in the time before the Reformation. Recent research has pointed out that there is significant evidence for theological and spiritual liveliness during that time.[11] By all odds, people were loyal to the Church; most of them conformed, either out of habit or conviction, to the external canons of expected ecclesiastical demeanor. Speaking about the Reformation in that context suggests that there is no a priori reason to assume that society was particularly predisposed to embrace a religious mass movement in its midst.

A second presupposition entails the argument that the Reformation was religious in name only and expressed, in a fundamental sense, political and social concerns. If such an argument is correct, the state of piety and religion is relatively unimportant, and the focus of our attention must be the awareness of a possible crisis in early sixteenth-century society, particularly, of course, in Germany, where the movement erupted.

In either case—the presupposition of the Reformation as a religious movement or as a political one—a further caveat is very much in order. To study the Reformation as a popular movement means that our focus is on nameless men and women whose impact upon the historical process, while surely real, never attained the credential of individuality. It is clear that the real decisions in the age of the Reformation were made not by "crowds," but by leaders who may have ignored them (if they indeed ubiquitously existed) or used them for their own particular purposes. The English Reformation story, in other words, finds its explanation more in the powerful and all-embracing figure of Henry VIII than in the happenings in the inns and alehouses of Cambridge.

The exploration of the popular dimension of the Reformation, moreover, is not unlike that of the psychopathological characteristics of the great historical figure. We know what happened, how the Reformation proceeded, how things turned out in the end. Our investigation will only ask some questions and, in so doing, demand greater precision for the generalizations made. The elephant may give birth to a mouse. Accordingly, we must not overestimate the significance of our topic in terms of the unfolding of events in the sixteenth century.

*   *   *   *

Before turning from the lofty heights of theoretical reflection to the specific realities of historical investigation, we must yet explore why, finally, our topic is insoluble. The fact of the matter is that several methodological problems stand in the way of its successful analysis.

For one, there is the complexity of quantified data. To offer this observation constitutes no startling revelation; I make mention of it merely to underscore the import of methodological considerations. The assertions of ten patricians tell us something different about the ideological constellation in a community in the early Reformation than do those of ten artisans. In the matrix of social and intellectual history (with which we are here concerned), ten do not always equal ten. C.-P. Clasen's otherwise significant *Anabaptism: A Social History* raises questions precisely at this point, in that it appears to be overawed with the import of statistical data about the sixteenth-century Anabaptists which is, upon scrutiny, most severely limited.[12] Obsession with quantifiable data can easily lead to a myth of objectivity, a myth because (as far as the early sixteenth century is concerned) the data ignore the fragmentary, even accidental character of the evidence, and slight the necessity of imposing qualitative judgments on quantitative findings. I find it an altogether open question whether completeness of the evidence (say, plebiscites in every community or territory accepting the Reformation) would tell us incisively more about the nature of the movement than we know now. We need only remind ourselves that the twentieth-century historian has such complete evidence, and yet our study of the Nazi movement or postwar American society is surely not beyond uncertainty and controversy.

Moreover, our topic needs specificity. The Reformation was

a movement of European significance and extended over several decades. A phenomenon that reached from England to Transylvania, from Finland to Italy, that began in 1517 and did not end until about three generations later makes the precariousness of sweeping generalizations all too obvious.[13] Indeed, this geographically and chronologically diverse scene also was heterogeneous in terms of its inner dynamic. The situation was hardly uniform throughout the length and breadth of Europe. What may be said about the movement in one specific instance at one specific place does not necessarily hold true for others. To talk about the popular dimension of "the" Reformation is thus difficult. Historians will benefit from a more differentiated definition of what we mean by "Reformation," and yet, no matter what that definition may be, the problem of the popular dimension remains complex and important.

The ambiguity of the term "Reformation" is matched by the evasiveness of the term "popular dimension." Whatever definitions come to mind, all have in common the fact that they suggest a positive response among the people to the proclamation of the reformers. Two complications arise. One has to do with the difficulty of speaking precisely of the meaning of this "response";[14] the other has to do with quantifying it.

Such terms as "response," "popular dimension," and "echo" are singularly vague. They may refer to the intellectual assent to specific affirmations propounded by the reformers—though what these affirmations were must yet be established. "Response" may also mean an emotional commitment to general notions of "reform."

Moreover, questions arise as to how such "response" becomes a movement, and how a movement becomes a *popular* movement? Does it happen through the intensity of conviction of its adherents or the attainment of a certain percentage of the population? If the former, is it measurable, and, if the latter, what is the context of our reflections? Also, there are subtle arithmetic difficulties. Do we fix that percentage at 10% or 50% of the population? Such questions are not easily answered.

There are considerable methodological difficulties, and the question remains whether the possibilities permitted by the sources allow us significant insights.

* * * *

The present essay attempts to explore the evidence for the popular dimension of the Reformation. It will concentrate on Germany, though it will make comments about other European countries as well, thereby venturing certain summary statements of general European significance. Our chronological scope is the *early* Reformation, the years of storm and stress, that period between the outbreak of the controversy and the formal acceptance of the new Protestant faith in a given locale. Thereby we focus on the crucial period of transition, when the old, in a striking manner, gave way to the new.

The most obvious type of source material consists of personal testimonials to the impact of the new faith, the acknowledgement, now bold, now hesitant, of being a partisan of the new gospel. Thomas Müntzer, for example, eloquently announced that he was a "messenger of Luther," while Albrecht Dürer plaintively affirmed that Luther helped him to understand the meaning of the gospel.[15] Lazarus Spengler spoke of himself as "erben liebhabers göttlicher warhait."[16] These testimonials convey, in one form or another, the meaning of the new proclamation for these individuals. Others could easily be cited.[17] We have many such testimonials—some touching, others pedestrian; some simple, others elaborate. Their relatively easy availability, however, must not lead us to overlook that, when measured against the populace at large, their number is insignificant.[18] There are some obvious reasons for this. As a rule, the sources give us only the pronouncements of men and women (mainly men, of course) who occupied positions of eminence in the unfolding course of events. The common people fell by the wayside, and, as far as the historical record is concerned, we may make surmises but have few facts. Only in one segment of the Reformation do these personal testimonials encompass common folk as well—in the Anabaptist fringe of the Reformation, where the comprehensive attempt of the authorities to suppress the Anabaptist movement meant that evidence of this sort from the rank and file is extensive.[19] In relative as well as absolute figures, however, the number of Anabaptists was small, indeed; C.-P. Clasen's recent monograph totals some three thousand Anabaptists for the first ten years of the movement (1525–1535) for South Germany, which, given a population of three million, is hardly an impressive figure.[20]

* * * *

A second type of source consists of the observations made by contemporaries about the spread or presence of Lutheran (Reformation) ideas in a given locale or among certain people. Such observations come from both antagonists and partisans of the New Faith, the only difference being, of course, that the former bewailed and the latter praised the events described.[21] All of these sources view men and events subjectively. They convey the observers' personal point of view, raising questions about their aspirations to perceptiveness as well as omniscience. Thus the comment of a chronicler that "in the year 1524 Martin Luther's heretical seed spread greatly in all places" entitles us to a measure of doubt concerning his evidence.[22] Erasmus purported to similar insight: "All of England is excited about Martin Luther," he wrote from London in 1520. Without doubting his sincerity, we can be less sure of his competent knowledge concerning the excitement of "all of England."[23] On another occasion, Erasmus spoke about "those who agree with Luther" and added intriguingly "and that includes all men of good will." Undoubtedly he meant to convey an impression, but of what (the observer or the scene) is not evident. In any case, the authenticity of the observation is not to be taken for granted.

Some observations appear more informed because more restricted, as when Christoph Scheurl wrote from Nuremberg that "most of the merchants here regret the use of force against Luther."[24] Of a similar character also are various governmental observations, such as the official comment, made in Nuremberg, that the Lutheran preaching occurred "before a great many people,"[25] or the observation made in Ansbach that people had stopped going to church.[26]

Related are the various official pronouncements (mainly from opponents of the reforming cause) concerning the spread of the Lutheran "disease." We must keep in mind, however, that here the focus of concern generally was more the intensity than the dimensions of the movement. In any case, a great number of such pronouncements are available, suggesting that the authorities were aware of the impact of the movement. The Nuremberg City Council, for example, informed Ferdinand of Austria in 1524 that if the anti-Lutheran mandate of the Imperial Regiment were enforced, rebellion, bloodshed, and disaster would result.[27]

Collectively these observations leave us in the dark as to the empirical reality corresponding to the nations in the observers' minds. We may conclude only that a long catena of statements uniformly and emphatically affirms the impact of the new proclamation upon people and society.

*   *   *   *

A third type of evidence may be found in the dissemination of "Lutheran" books and pamphlets in the early Reformation. The term "Lutheran" must be put into quotation marks here in order to denote that the publications were Lutheran only in a broad and general sense. They hardly offered a compendium of Lutheran dogmatic theology. Their main characteristic was vagueness. They vaguely echoed Luther's notions, expressed ecclesiastical concern, or advocated change. The invention of printing had a formidable impact upon the Reformation in the most fundamental sense possible.[28] The printed page provided a revolutionary means to disseminate ideas—not only in a small circle of the initiated, but among all those who could read.

Significantly, many bits of evidence attest to the dissemination of Lutheran tracts throughout Germany.[29] Having made this remark, we must repeat what we have already noted with respect to the first two types of evidence, namely that persuasive findings are difficult to obtain.[30] The problem lies in our haphazard and thus limited knowledge of the size of the individual editions of a book or pamphlet. We are hardly in a position, therefore, to offer conclusive statements concerning the number of copies in circulation at a given time.

There is firm ground to begin with: the number of published titles. In Germany the number of vernacular reform publications on theological and devotional topics increased significantly in the decade after 1518, a fact which becomes useful evidence for establishing the impact of the new proclamation.[31] The religious pamphlets created a new genre of publication with their emphasis on brevity and their use of the vernacular. Luther himself published some fifty separate titles between 1517 and 1524, and his reforming colleagues were no less eager to burst into print.

Uncertainty prevails, however, as soon as we attempt to calculate the actual number of copies in circulation on the basis of the titles published. Only conjectures may be offered. If we assume one thousand copies per publication, as has been suggested, the total number of copies of "Martinian" books in circulation in Germany by 1524 would come to something like one and one-half million.[32] This is, by all odds, the maximum figure. In itself impressive, the figure is made even more so when viewed against a population of about fifteen million.

But difficulties remain. The evidence concerning the dissemination of books and pamphlets by no means establishes automatically an impact of the ideas promulgated.[33] Obviously a distinction must be made between the mere purchase of a book and concurrence with its ideas. A book bought is not necessarily a book read, even as a book read is not always a book endorsed. Few of us would claim that the astronomical figures of the dissemination of the Bible in our own day (notably in motel rooms) say much, if anything, about current religious interest. In the early 1520's plain curiosity may well have entered the picture, and thus the raw data do not necessarily provide an infallible clue to the existence of a large following.

On their face, however, the figures are impressive. They show, at the very least, that the cause of reform attained a striking interest in Germany in the mid-1520's. At the same time, the determination of the political authorities to suppress Lutheran literature would indicate that they, too, acknowledged (and combated) its widespread dissemination.[34]

* * * *

Another type of evidence is found in the testamentary bequests made to ecclesiastical causes in the period between the outbreak of the Reformation and the formal acceptance of the New Faith. This specific chronological delimitation is important, for it may be argued that the true impact of the new proclamation found expression precisely during that time when the formal structures of the Catholic Church continued to exist, but the advocacy of reform notions suggested individual departure from such existing formal standards. Again, difficulties remain, since many uncertainties are very much part of the picture.[35] Thus testamentary bequests presuppose wealth; they can come only from a minute section of the population whose attitudes may not be those of the populace as a whole.

We note that testamentary bequests for ecclesiastical causes do not show—contrary to widely held generalizations—any marked decrease in the time immediately preceding the Reformation. The rate of such giving held its own. Pre-Reformation evidence thus suggests an undiminished loyalty on the part of the people—at least the more prosperous element of the populace—to the Catholic Church.

To establish the full pattern of ecclesiastical bequests after the beginning of the Reformation will require extensive studies. In this essay I must depend on first impressions, based on select archival researches and available printed sources.

The available data suggest that the pattern of virtually unchanged ecclesiastical bequests in the years immediately before the Reformation disappeared as soon as the religious controversy broke out. Bequests declined significantly, reaching zero as soon as the New Faith was formally introduced. In Nuremberg the last ecclesiastical bequest was made in 1523, with the years after 1505 showing the following distribution:[36]

1505–1509	7
1510–1514	9
1515–1519	6
1520–1524	3
1525 ff.	0

For Hildesheim the figures are as follows:[37]

1500–1509	18
1510–1519	18
1520–1529	9 (plus eight bequests for charitable purposes)
1530–1539	3 (plus four bequests for charitable purposes)

Studies of English wills, focusing on the slightly different though corollary aspect of the traditional ecclesiastical form rather than on the content of the bequests, have conveyed a similar picture.[38] In Yorkshire in 1538–1540, nine out of seventy-eight wills were of a non-traditional (i.e., Protestant) form. Ten years later the two forms were about equal (twenty-three versus twenty-four), and the entire period of 1538–1552 is characterized by a balance between traditional and non-traditional wills.

Two explanations suggest themselves for the decline in giving during the period from the beginning of the Reformation, on the one hand, to its formal adoption in a community, on the other. Appearance during the pre-Reformation period notwithstanding, authentic loyalty to the Church may have been precarious, prompting an abrupt decline in ecclesiastical bequests as soon as the controversy erupted, even if—and this is important—it was not accompanied by an acceptance of the new proclamation. A second explanation would be that the appeal of the Reformation message was persuasive, compelling those who were formally still Catholics to draw practical consequences from their new religious stance. The increase in charitable bequests after the outbreak of the Reformation—while ecclesiastical bequests declined—may be seen as indirect confirmation of this interpretation.[39]

A related matter is the involvement of the people in formal Catholic rites during this same transitional period. Contemporaries tend to note that popular involvement in Catholic observances decreased significantly. In Frankfurt, for example, public processions in 1526 were recorded by the chronicler as having had fewer participants—"ist wenig folk mitgangen"—while he observed for 1527 "hat das gemein folk vil mormelns und gespoet gehabt."[40]

* * * *

Then there is the evidence of the cities. Bernd Moeller's study on *The Imperial Cities and the Reformation* has called attention to the close correlation between the acceptance of the Reformation and the extent of popular participation in municipal affairs.[41] Indeed, the imperial cities emerge as a useful thermometer for the popular dimension of the Reformation. We may place the evidence regarding popular sentiment into the framework of the actual outcome of events, the formal acceptance of the New Faith in the overwhelming majority of the cities. Together, agitation and outcome suggest certain probabilities concerning the popular appeal of the Reformation message.

The evidence available for the cities is of two sorts—one pertaining to the involvement of the city councils or guild representatives, the other to that of the populace at large.

As regards the former, we may note that most of the city council members of Breslau were by 1523 of Lutheran orientation.[42] Similarly, council elections in Halle in 1534 saw, with a single exception, Lutheran members successful.[43] In Basel the guilds submitted a petition to the council to permit only the new proclamation in the city.[44] The city council decision to remove the images from the churches was virtually unanimous.[45] The guilds generally played an important role.[46]

In Dortmund, only four of twenty-four representatives of the guilds were loyal Catholics in 1527.[47] In Görlitz, the guild of weavers, which comprised one-sixth of the population, formally opted for the New Faith.[48] Half of the council members in Lubeck favored the Reformation. On the other hand, the 1525 decision of the Large Council in Zurich to abolish the Mass had a majority "of a few hands"; two years later one observer surmised that some thirty to forty "enemies" of the Reformation could still be found in the Large Council—out of two hundred members![49]

The evidence for the popular sentiment is more sporadic. From several cities we know that the sermons of reform-minded ministers were received by enthusiastic crowds.[50] In Nuremberg, for example, St. Sebald's Church was so overcrowded that the city council ordered the installation of an additional balcony.[51] In some instances the formal introduction of the New Faith was made dependent on actual votes. In Solothurn two votes were taken in 1529 regarding the religious issue. In the first of these, nineteen parishes opted for the old faith and fifteen for the new, while thirteen were willing to let the authorities decide. A second vote brought these figures to twenty-two, twenty, and ten respectively.[52] A slightly different type of evidence comes from Ulm, where in 1530 some 87% of the burghers opposed the Augsburg recess.[53] That vote clearly constitutes a different type of evidence, because the Augsburg recess also was a political document, and response to it could be explicitly motivated by other than religious considerations.[54] But the question of motivation, naggingly lurking behind our investigation, may be excluded. Whatever the reason for the support of Luther and reform, we are concerned only with its reality. In Esslingen, some 142 out of 1,076 burghers voted against ecclesiastical change.[55] In Ravensburg, a communal decision heralded the formal introduction of the Reformation.[56] In Lubeck, the burghers "voted" with their lungs, as it were, by a "sing-in" of the new "Lutheran" hymns.[57] In Basel, an armed crowd of 3,000 (out of a population of 16,000!) demonstrated on behalf of the New Faith.[58]

The evidence from the cities is, in short, the most extensive we have. Still, we must not ignore its restricted character. The evidence of actual popular sentiment must be distinguished from that of municipal councils. Even a unanimous council decision in favor of the New Faith says nothing about popular opinion. Above all, it points to the notion of a *Ratsreformation,* a reform through council, without indicating the sentiment of the population.[59] We may conjecture, all the same, that even a blatantly political action of a council occurred with the awareness that this action would be acceptable to the citizenry, thus at the very least suggesting a positive climate of opinion. But we must also recall the chronic tensions between councils and the guilds (and burghers!) with respect to the issue of religious reform.[60] Indeed, historians have paid increasing attention to the political elites which played a crucial role in the unfolding of the urban Reformation. Both Bernd Moeller's study and the more specific researches of M. Chrisman, Robert Walton, Leonhard von Muralt, and Walter Jacob have focused on the internal structural dynamics of formal ecclesiastical change.[61] Clearly the Reformation message did find entry into the sociopolitical structures, affecting the course of society and indicating a measure of popular appeal.[62]

*   *   *   *

Another type of evidence for the popular dimension of the New Faith is found in the instances of the disruption of law and order that occurred in the early Reformation. Such disruption must be seen as an important element.

The fact of the matter is that the religious controversy frequently took the form of civil disturbances—iconoclasms, rioting, demonstrations. It did so with almost stereotyped monotony. Any study of the Reformation in the cities must include such turbulences as altogether typical occurrences. There were dozens of them—in Wittenberg in 1521, in Zurich in 1523, in Basel in 1528, and in St. Gall in 1529, to name but a few. However, they probably affected only a small portion of the populace, and the significance of evidence of this kind may lie more in the demonstration of the intensity of the conviction than of its extent.[63]

The most spectacular expression of the convergence of Reformation and disruption of society is generally said to have been the uprising of the German peasants in 1524–1525. It may be viewed as a dramatic manifestation of the coming together of Reformation ideas and popular sentiment. The point of reference is the *Twelve Articles*, the only published document of peasants' demands, which embodied the juxtaposition of Lutheran religion and social reform, bedecked with Biblical passages. The conclusion seems obvious that the popular impact of the Reformation is demonstrated by the peasants' uprising.

The situation, however, is quite complicated. Other evidence coming from the numerous unpublished peasant grievance documents suggests that the approach of the *Twelve Articles* was not echoed by other peasants in the uprising, even though the *Articles* were widely reprinted.[64] As a rule, these documents were concerned with matters at once immediate and specific; they deal with very tangible economic and social issues. Religious grievances are virtually nonexistent, and even the religious ornamentation of socio-economic demands is rare. Accordingly, this evidence does not provide us with sufficiently helpful clues as to the role of religion in the minds of the insurgents. The *Twelve Articles*, in short, may have been an altogether unrepresentative document.

This takes us to the assertion of Marxist historiography that the Reformation, occurring in the setting of the conflict between two economic systems, was borne in by the representatives of the new system, i.e. the early bourgeoisie. While this view is impressive for its over-arching theme, to relate it to the empirical evidence is not easy. Accordingly, Marxist historians of Early Modern Europe have had a good deal of difficulty arriving at a common perspective in their particular interpretation of the evidence. M. M. Smirin has argued that the early bourgeoisie was involved on the side of the peasants, while Max Steinmetz found that the peasants played an important role as the "fighting" arm of the bourgeoisie.[65] All of them do insist, however, on the close connection between the Reformation and the turbulence of the 1520's, subsuming both under the heading of "Early

Bourgeois Revolution," and viewing them as a significant popular phenomenon.

From the perspective of this paper—which is concerned with the popular dimension of the Reformation, not with the ideological identity of socio-economic groups and classes—this view raises the problem that, even though there was a very strong appeal in Reformation literature to the peasant and to social issues,[66] the evidence for an extensive manifestation of religious concerns by the rebelling peasants is slender. There can be no doubt, of course, that the Peasants' War did constitute an extensive popular phenomenon. We should doubt, however, that it may be subsumed under the Reformation. It seems more appropriate to speak of the Reformation as having precipitated a mass movement rather than to identify it with one. Many of the "reforming" ministers in the towns spoke against the uprising.[67]

Moreover, the other major uprising of the time in which religious and secular motivations intertwined—the "Pilgrimage of Grace"—expressed a conservative, Catholic sentiment.[68] If we see the Pilgrimage in the same context as historians have seen the German Peasants' War, namely, a Reformation setting giving rise to a socio-religious movement, then it becomes rather baffling as far as the religious sentiments of the people are concerned.

* * * *

Finally, we must briefly cite the presence of a "reform" minister in a community as an indicator, however indirect, of popular sentiment. Of these, there were dozens upon dozens in Germany.[69] If anything, the demand for a preacher "to proclaim the pure 'Word of God'" constituted the basic element in the course of Reformation events. Generally, the reforming ministers received expressions of popular support in the face of hostile authorities or city council.[70] The presence of such clergy in a community in itself establishes nothing more than a possibility, but the fact remains that people were directly exposed to the constant proselytizing influence of a leadership figure.[71]

Such exposure occurred daily, and it is easy to imagine a popular ramification of the proclamation in such a setting.[72]

*   *   *   *

Thus far our comments have focused on the closely circumscribed setting of the imperial free cities and territories in Germany. At this point a word is in order about the European scene. Our difficulties with the sources, particularly with regard to the need to relate the part to the whole, increase immensely. The European sources flow sparingly. A few comments from London or Cambridge hardly suffice as observations for all of England. The German riddle becomes, to use Churchillian prose, an English (or French, or Swedish) enigma wrapped in a mystery. Few studies are available, and most, such as that of Frederick Heymann on Bohemia or Franz Petri on the Low Countries, stress the existence of vernacular translations of Luther or the presence of individual reform-minded clergy.[73] Little is said about the people.

Since I myself offer no particular expertise in European sources, my remarks are meant to be impressionistic rather than comprehensive. Among several important aspects of the matter, I should like to note first the chronological disparity between events in Germany and those elsewhere in Europe. The various European countries did not face the issue of the Reformation at the same point in time, some of them in a real sense not until the middle of the century. This means that our use of evidence of literacy or printing must take chronological variance into consideration. Moreover, if we have noted that the quantity of sources is much smaller for the other European countries than for Germany, part of the explanation lies in the absence of the equivalent to the free cities, where internal agitation had the potential of leading to legally viable change. In the German imperial cities the legal situation allowed for direct involvement on the part of the political authorities. Since the empirical setting was small, there exists more extensive documentation of the process of change.

And something else. Some time ago I suggested that the dissemination of the Reformation differed qualitatively in Germany and the European countries on account of the divergent roles played by propaganda materials.[74] In Germany the flood of vernacular *Flugschriften* occurred almost at the outset of the controversy and allowed for an extensive spread of the new ideas. Elsewhere in Europe this vernacular outpouring did not exist at the beginning. The vernacular religious publications in France prior to 1540 were fewer than were published in Germany prior to 1520; the figures for England, while slightly different, are analogous to those of France.[75] Accordingly, there is little reason to expect that the new ideas were disseminated from the beginning as dramatically in the rest of Europe as they had been in Germany.

Generally, we have little evidence. We must not assume a conspiracy of silence in the sources, nor the systematic destruction of relevant documents, nor need we anticipate that a new generation of historians, more industrious than our own, or blessed with better methods, will obtain findings that will bring into bright sunlight what presently slumbers in darkness.[76] It simply is not conceivable that the common people in Norwich or Canterbury, Amiens or Autun, could have attained any authentic information about the new religious ideas discussed in Germany other than in the vaguest of terms, the way they were informed about strange peoples and customs. In other words, during the early phase of the Reformation in England, France, or Sweden, the movement could not possess a popular dimension, unless we are disposed to employ a definition of the Reformation—quite in accord with Lucien Febvre's essay[77]—that makes it impossible to define a specific literature or message of reform, and moreover ignores the German stimulus, direct as well as indirect, for the outbreak of the controversy. There was random knowledge, sporadic curiosity, and occasional enthusiasm. The many accounts about the involvement of the common people told by John Foxe, in his *Book of Martyrs*, do not disprove this point, nor does similar evidence from other countries.[78] The group gathering at the White Horse Tavern in Cambridge to talk about the latest in the theological *haut monde* hardly qualifies as evidence for widespread popular enthusiasm for a new form of Christian spirituality.

If these remarks are characterized by accuracy as well as persuasiveness, we may conclude not only that the popular dimension of the Reformation had to be limited but also that the subsequent role of the local clergy as propagators of the New Faith (and the concomitant creators of a popular impact) was crucial. The increase in popular support for the Reformation in various European countries was a slow process, burdened, after all, by the fact that enthusiasm had to be forged at a time when the Reformation movement in general had already been discredited for its heretical stance. Only with the emergence of an indigenous religious literature and the ubiquitous presence of reform-minded clergy did the situation change.

With this comment we may build a bridge between the assertion that there could not be any initial popular movement in countries other than Germany, on the one hand, and the obvious incidence of extensive controversy and agitation at various places, on the other. Not only did vernacular religious writings increasingly appear, but also the type of evidence described earlier in this essay becomes more frequent as the years pass. We have, for example, the same kind of generalizing observations: in Poland the claim was made in the middle of the century "that almost all distinguished families of Poland have joined the sectarians."[79] More specific data are also available. Visitation records of 1565–1570, for example, suggest that in Minor Poland about one-seventh of the parishes were Protestant.[80] Estimates of the strength of Protestantism in France indicate that one-tenth of the populace was Protestant in the 1560's.[81]

* * * *

I conclude and ask what summary statements emerge from the evidence and our reflections. I should like to enumerate them as follows:

1. There is evidence for extensive religious agitation, evidence also for an endorsement of Reform ideas by certain seg-

ments of society. It is incorrect to assert that the religious controversy during the period was marginal. People were also concerned about the Turkish danger or the French disease, about the weather or children, about timeless no less than time-conditioned topics; the religious controversy, however, was very much in the center of things.

2. There is no direct evidence for a comprehensive popular echo, going through all strata of society, of the reformers' proclamation. The available evidence does not allow the clear conclusion that the German Reformation, even in its early phase, was a mass movement.

3. The evidence generally is sporadic, random, and incomplete.

4. Unanimously, all observers, speaking about individuals or groups, agree that the spread of the "Lutheran evangel" or "pestilence" (depending on the stance of the reporter) was formidable. No contemporary observer, not even the staunchest Catholic, denied the significant impact of the Reformation.

5. The sources are virtually silent about the sentiment of the common people, the men and women in the pews or on the street. What happened in the villages of Franconia or Devonshire, or the streets of Ulm or Cambridge may only be inferred.

It is clear that to talk about all of early sixteenth-century society tends to bestow a certain status upon some strata which, in actual fact, did not possess it. To the extent to which society was not in the hands of the authorities, only the nobility and the cities were forces to be reckoned with. While individual circumstances may vary, the overall conclusion surely must be that society has to be defined selectively rather than comprehensively. This is especially true for those elements, notably the peasants, who lived in their own world, so to speak, and had little active involvement in society at large. To be sure, Thomas More's controversial work makes significant claims to insight even on this level. But questions remain.

6. The quantitative dimension of the popular impact is difficult to establish. In a few instances the evidence is explicit in that we have the actual votes of the citizenry in favor of the new

interpretation of the gospel, a fact which surely allows us to think that over 50% of the voters were for innovation. But such instances are exceptions. We are unable to place the evidence in a larger setting. We simply do not know, in most instances, the ratio of partisans of the New Faith to either the *active* population at large or to the active partisans of the Old Faith. As a rule, we have the testimonials of the former without being aware of the dimensions of the latter. The two must be considered conjointly; the one without the other is meaningless. Even those of us who are disposed to look with disdain on the quantifiers among the historians must acknowledge that fifty testimonials out of a hundred indicate something different from fifty out of a thousand. The petition of fifteen "Lutheran" burghers in Regensburg in 1524 for Communion under both kinds serves as a good case in point. At that time Regensburg had some 6,000–10,000 inhabitants; the problem is how to relate these two figures meaningfully.[82]

7. The matter comes down to two important considerations. The one has to do with the interpretation of the unquestionably meager evidence. Several possibilities exist, each leading to a different conclusion concerning the popular dimension of the Reformation. The other relates to our understanding of the general setting of the early sixteenth century. Was society in a crisis? Was there yearning for religious and ecclesiastical or even societal reform? Depending on how we answer these questions, our specific understanding of the Reformation as a popular movement will be affected.

8. The number of active partisans of the Reformation was confined to less than a majority of the population. The Solothurn survey, which suggests an almost even division between the adherents of the Old and the New Faith, appears more representative of the actual sentiment than do the figures pertaining to the unanimous acceptance of the New Faith in Geneva.

The evidence for the persistence of Catholic loyalty both preceding and following the outbreak of the Reformation should be considered here. The general uncertainty as to the true nature of the controversy which prevailed for several years must have enhanced the quantitative dimension of the movement in that support was possible without taking a definitive stand against the Catholic Church. After 1525 such fluidity ceased to exist, and the full awareness of the implications of supporting Luther became obvious. The clear evidence for a widespread retention of Catholic loyalty must be deemed important.

9. Finally, there is the possibility that the controversy was perceived as touching on matters other than religion and that the popular response derived its momentum precisely from such a non-religious perception. We are unable to read people's minds and discern true conviction behind the facade of external protestations. To say this is neither a novel nor a profound insight. We cannot say why people joined Luther's camp. We may offer only surmises—noting that the causes of the movement were economic, political, or religious, or that any of these merely provided the ideology for the truly authentic cause.

Having said this, we must observe that it makes little difference for the historical course of events whether the adherents of a movement correctly perceive its purpose. The historian will be curious to know exactly what agitated the rank and file, but even in the absence of such knowledge the fact that they were agitated intimates a significant congruence of ideas and events.

In closing I must return to my initial remark that the topic of the popular dimension of the Reformation is "seemingly crucial" for our understanding of the Reformation. The attentive reader will no doubt have noticed my caution, both here and elsewhere. It arises out of more than a concern to cover all exits; it constitutes a caveat that the blatantly meager conclusions of this essay be put into proper perspective. My simple point is that the Reformation historian must be precise as well as cautious with his claims. He must research, analyze, examine, but in so doing pay careful attention to the exact availability of sources. If the sources are silent, the conclusions must so indicate. That, too, constitutes an insight, even as it leaves a niche, however small, for the historian's imagination.

Notes

1. The best summary is that of O. H. Pesch, "Zur Frage nach Luthers reformatorischer Wende," in B. Lohse, ed., *Der Durchbruch der reformatorischen Erkenntnis bei Luther* (Darmstadt, 1968), pp. 445–505.

2. J. T. McNeill, "The Religious Initiative in Reformation History," in J. C. Brauer, ed., *The Impact of the Church upon Its Culture* (Chicago, 1968), pp. 173–207, is useful for its emphasis on the significance of religious ideas and notions in the Reformation.

3. R. Walton has a splendid study of Zurich: "The Institutionalization of the Reformation at Zurich," *Zwingliana*, 13 (1972), 497–515. On Nuremberg see G. Pfeiffer, "Die Einführung der Reformation in Nürnberg," *Bl. f. dt. Landesgeschichte*, 89 (1952), 112–133.

4. The classic repudiation of the notion of the loss of popular support is the essay by F. Lau, "Der Bauernkrieg und das angebliche Ende der lutherischen Reformation als spontaner Volksbewegung," *Luther-Jahrbuch*, 26 (1959), 109–134. L. Spitz, *The Renaissance and Reformation Movements* (Chicago, 1971), p. 346, argues differently that only *after* (!) the failure of the revolt "did the peasants turn to Luther's evangelical religion en masse."

5. Actual studies on the popular impact of the Reformation are few, notably G. Vogler, "Reformation und Volksbewegung—Ein Forschungsproblem," in M. Steinmetz and G. Brendler, eds., *Weltwirkung der Reformation* (Berlin, 1969), pp. 251–262; R. B. Manning, "The Spread of the Popular Reformation in England," *Sixteenth Century Essays and Studies* (St. Louis, 1970), pp. 35–52. An interesting study on a related topic is K. Czok, "Revolutionäre Volksbewegungen in mitteldeutschen Städten zur Zeit von Reformation und Bauernkrieg," in L. Stern and M. Steinmetz, eds., *450 Jahre Reformation* (Berlin, 1967), pp. 128–146. There are, of course, a formidable number of monographic studies on the Reformation in towns and territories, but few of them deal explicitly and in detail with the popular movement. Recent studies tend to show a greater concern, but even then the quantitative basis often remains rather limited. Thus N. L. Roelker's essay, "The Appeal of Calvinism to French Noblewomen in the Sixteenth Century," *Journal of Interdisciplinary History*, 2 (1972), 391–418, includes only some fifty names.

6. The most accessible introduction to Marxist historiography is R. Wohlpfeil, ed., *Reformation oder Frühbürgerliche Revolution* (Munich, 1972). M. Steinmetz speaks (*ibid.*, p. 59) of a "Bewegung nationalen Ausmasses" and a "Volksreformation."

7. H. J. Grimm, *The Reformation Era 1500–1650* (New York, 1973; first ed., 1954), p. 1; J. M. Todd, *Reformation* (New York, 1971), p. 196; J. P. Dolan, *History of the Reformation* (New York, 1965), p. 273.

8. H. J. Hillerbrand, *The World of the Reformation* (New York, 1973), p. 37.

9. B. Moeller, *Imperial Cities and the Reformation* (Philadelphia, 1972), p. 41; W. P. Fuchs in B. Gebhardt, *Handbuch der Deutschen Geschichte* (Stuttgart, 1955), II, 38. See also G. Schramm, *Der polnische Adel und die Reformation 1548–1607* (Wiesbaden, 1965), p. 319. Schramm sees the "Reformation against the will of the ruler" as one type of the European Reformation.

10. I am impressed, for example, by the data in "Bishop Hooper's Visitation of Gloucester," ed. James Gairdner, *English Historical Review*, 19 (1904), 98–122. The important monograph of J. Toussaert, *La Sentiment religieux en Flandre à la fin du Moyen Age* (Paris, 1960), finds an appalling disinterest and illiteracy in matters of religion, a finding which, on a broader geographic scale, is confirmed for the sixteenth and seventeenth centuries by J. Delumeau, *Le Catholicisme*

Hans J. Hillerbrand

entre Luther et Voltaire (Paris, 1971). The best bibliographical survey of visitation sources is found in K. Eder, *Die landesfürstliche Visitation von 1544/1545 in der Steiermark; ein Beitrag zur Reformationsgeschichte Innerösterreichs* (Graz, 1955).

11. B. Moeller, "Frömmigkeit in Deutschland um 1500," *Archiv f. Reformationsgesch.*, 56 (1965), 5–30. Moeller's attempt to analyze pre-Reformation piety in Germany has its necessary corollary in the definition of the Reformation as a movement of popular piety.

12. C.-P. Clasen, *Anabaptism: A Social History, 1525–1618* (Ithaca, 1972).

13. The otherwise valuable dissertation of A. O. Hancock, "The Reformation in Hesse to 1538" (Emory University, 1962), omits any reference—however passing —to the popular impact of the Reformation movement. The same applies to G. Carlsson, "Preussischer Einfluss auf die Reformation Schwedens," *Beiträge z. deutschen und nordischen Geschichte* (Schleswig, 1952), pp. 36–48, or to H. Buck and E. Fabian, *Konstanzer Reformationsgeschichte* (Tubingen, 1965), to name but two studies at random.

14. I find myself most intrigued, as regards both methodology and content, by the study of J. Toussaert, *op. cit.*, and the more general studies of Fr. Rapp, *L'Église et la vie religieuse en occident à la fin du Moyen Age* (Paris, 1971), and of B. Moeller, *op. cit.* The methodology employed in these and other studies entails an attempt either at quantification (of what is often unquantifiable) or at imaginative inferences. Our topic approximates, but is not identical with, the generic study of popular religion, as proposed, for example, by N. Z. Davis, "Some Tasks and Themes in the Study of Popular Religion," in C. Trinkaus and H. A. Oberman, eds., *The Pursuit of Holiness in Late Medieval and Renaissance Religion* (Leiden, 1974), pp. 307–338. Professor Davis is concerned with rejecting the distinction between superstition and religion, "acceptable" and "non-acceptable" forms of spirituality and piety. She sees the *raison d'être* for each in its historical existence. The short time span within which we confine this study (the first few years of the Reformation) will preclude significant yields from the methodology espoused by Professor Davis.

15. Extensive references to such testimonials are found in R. Fife, *The Revolt of Martin Luther* (New York, 1957), pp. 415 ff.

16. H. v. Schubert, *Lazarus Spengler und die Reformation in Nürnberg* (Leipzig, 1934), p. 189.

17. Thus Ulrich Zasius called Luther the "Phoenix" of theologians and assured him that all theologians would follow him, *WA Br*, 2, p. 181. Interestingly enough, Zasius subsequently remained a loyal Catholic! Helius Eobanus Hessus wrote four elegies in Luther's honor (Carl Krause, *Helius Eobanus Hessus* [Gotha, 1879], II, 325).

18. For expressions of ignorance about the extent of popular impact, see J. R. Dieterich, *Reformationsgeschichte von Oppenheim* (Darmstadt, 1904), p. 38; K. Schornbaum, *Die Einführung der Reformation in der Stadt Hersbruck* (Munich, 1928), p. 25.

19. These testimonials are published in the impressive *Täufer-Akten* series (*Quellen zur Geschichte der Täufer*), now in fifteen volumes, published by the Verein für Reformationsgeschichte in Germany.

20. C.-P. Clasen, *op. cit.*, p. 26. According to Clasen the figures for Tyrol and Wurttemberg are .4% and .03%, respectively.

21. For Catholic comments see, e.g., K. Engelbert, "Die Anfänge der Lutherischen Bewegung in Breslau und Schlesien," *Archiv f. Schlesische Kirchengesch.*, 18 (1960), 147, 197; L. Arbusow, *Die Einführung der Reformation in Liv-, Est-,*

und Kurland (Leipzig, 1921), p. 207; G. Scholz, *Die Aufzeichnungen des Hildesheimer Dechanten Johan Oldecop 1493–1574* (Münster, 1972), p. 56, "de lutherischen friheit de overhaut genommen." See also the Nuremberg Council instruction, 1524: "die gemein zue Nuremberg zue dem wort Gottes gantz begierig" (G. Pfeiffer, *op. cit.*, p. 263).

22. C. Jager, "Reformationsgeschichte der Stadt Heilbronn und ihres ehemaligen Gebietes," *Mittheilungen zur schwäb. u. fränk. Reformationsgeschichte*, 1 (Stuttgart, 1828), 292. A similar comment comes from Appenzell, though in each instance the problem is the measure of accuracy: J. Willi, *Die Reformation im Lande Appenzell* (Bern, 1924), p. 36, "es gangend vill buechli und reden uss von einem, genant Martin Luther."

23. *Opus Epistolarum*, ed. P. S. Allen (Oxford, 1913), III, No. 967. Thomas More's polemical career tends to support Erasmus' contention. See, similarly, T. Schiess, ed., *Briefwechsel der Brüder Ambrosius und Thomas Blaurer* (Freiburg, 1912), III, 14.

24. F. v. Soden, ed., *Chr. Scheurl, Briefbuch* (Potsdam, 1867), II, 65.

25. *Deutsche Reichstagsakten*, JR (Gotha, 1893–1905), III, 414, "vor einer grossen menig volks gethan." J. Loserth, "Zu den Anfängen der Reformation in Steiermark," *Jahrb. d. Gesellschaft f. d. Geschichte der Protestantismus im ehem. u. im neuen Österreich*, 54 (1933), 85. See also *ibid.*, p. 86, for the report that the public reading of the anti-Lutheran mandates causes people to walk out of the church.

26. K. Schornbaum, "Zur religiösen Haltung der Stadt Ansbach," *Beitr. z. bayer. Kirchengesch.*, 7 (1901), 160.

27. Stadt-Archiv Nürnberg SI, L.30, Nr. 5.

28. See, notably, E. L. Eisenstein, "The Advent of Printing and the Protestant Revolt: A New Approach to the Disruption of Western Christendom," in R. Kingdon, ed., *Transition and Revolution* (Minneapolis, 1974), pp. 235 ff.

29. For example, K. Engelbert, *op. cit.*, p. 134; H. Haefliger, "Solothurn in der Reformation 1519–1534," *Jahrb. f. Solothurnische Gesch.*, 16 (1943), 31; *Deutsche Reichstagsakten*, JR IV, 496; W. Delius, *Die Reformationsgeschichte der Stadt Halle a. S.* (Berlin, 1953), p. 27; *Hanserecesse* III (Leipzig, 1870–1875), 9; W. Jannasch, *Reformationsgeschichte Lübecks vom Petersablass bis zum Augsburger Reichstag* (Lubeck, 1958), pp. 90, 125; J. Willi, *op. cit.*, p. 36; C. Krafft, "Über die Quellen der Geschichte der evangelischen Bewegungen am Niederrhein im 16ten Jahr hundert," *Theol. Arbeiten aus d. Rhein.-wissenschaftl. Predigerverein*, 1 (1872), 42, 44; P. Konrad, *Die Einführung der Reformation in Breslau und Schlesien* (Breslau, 1917), p. 15; E. Hahn, "Zur Appenzeller Reformationsgeschichte," *Zwingliana*, 1 (1897–1904), 375; W. F. Knoll, "Die Reformation in Lauf" (Diss., Erlangen, 1954), p. 60; J. Wipf, *Reformationsgeschichte der Stadt und Landschaft Schaffhausen* (Zurich, 1929), p. 174.

30. E. Eisenstein has perceptive observations on the whole range of issues, *op. cit.*, pp. 241 ff.

31. R. Crofts, "Ecclesiastical Reform Proposals in Germany from 1510 to 1520" (Diss., Duke University, 1969).

32. See L. Holborn, "Printing and the Growth of a Protestant Movement in Germany from 1517 to 1524," *Church History*, 11 (1942), 123–137. However, the evidence varies: Thomas Müntzer's tract entitled *Highly Provoked Defense and Answer* was printed in four hundred copies; see G. Pfeiffer, ed., *Quellen zur Nürnberger Reformationsgeschichte* (Nuremberg, 1968), p. 27.

33. Often the evidence is vague: *Deutsche Reichstagsakten*, JR IV, 480, "allerlei

Hans J. Hillerbrand

puchlin in geheimbd und unwissend durch frembde, unbekannte personen in unser statt." See also *ibid.*, p. 496.

34. See, for example, C. S. Meyer, "Henry VIII Burns Luther's Books, 12 May 1521," *Journal of Ecclesiastical History*, 9 (1958), 178.

35. See K. Eder, *Das Land ob der Enns vor der Glaubensspaltung* (Linz, 1932), I of the *Studien zur Reformationsgeschichte Oberösterreichs*. The tabulation of bequests for St. Pölten in Austria, from A. Scheiblin, "Reformation und Gegen-Reformation in St. Pölten," *Jahrbuch d. Gesellschaft f. Geschichte der Protestantismus im ehemaligen Österreich*, 62 (1941), 20, follows below:

	Total Number of Wills	Ecclesiastical Bequests		Non-Ecclesiastical Bequests	
1500–04	22	17	(77%)	5	(23%)
1505–09	43	33	(77%)	10	(23%)
1510–14	23	17	(74%)	6	(26%)
1515–19	35	32	(91%)	3	(9%)
1520–24	27	27	(100%)		
1525–29	22	17	(77%)	5	(23%)
1530–34	22	9	(41%)	13	(59%)
1535–39	21	12	(57%)	9	(43%)

T. Brodek, "Lay Community and Church Institutions of the Lahngau in the Late Middle Ages," *Central European History*, 2 (1969), 22–47, esp. p. 28, has tabulated donations for Limburg; the scarcity of data is once again evident. The figures cited for Augsburg by A. Werner, *Die örtlichen Stiftungen für die Zwecke des Unterrichts und der Wohltätigkeit in der Stadt Augsburg* (Augsburg, 1899), are too incomplete to be useful. While the variables are several and need to be considered, the use of wills as indices of popular piety may generally be taken for granted.

36. Stadtbibliothek Nürnberg, Handschrift Amb 17320.

37. R. Doebner, ed., *Urkundenbuch der Stadt Hildesheim* (Hildesheim, 1901).

38. The figures are found in A. G. Dickens, *Lollards and Protestants in the Diocese of York* (London, 1959), pp. 215 ff.

39. The decline in ecclesiastical bequests was also noted for Ansbach by K. Schornbaum, "Zur religiösen Haltung der Stadt Ansbach," *op. cit.*, p. 147.

40. J. Beumer, "Die Prozessionen im katholischen Frankfurt während der Reformationszeit," *Archiv f. mittelrh. Kirchengesch.*, 21 (1969), 109.

41. *Imperial Cities*, pp. 100 ff. The essay by J. M. Kittelson, "Wolfgang Capito, the Council, and Reform Strasbourg," *Archiv f. Reformationsgesch.*, 63 (1972), 126 f. shows, however, that in Strasbourg, in any case, the reforming clergy's appeal was to the *council* and not to the citizenry, indicating that they must have perceived either the real locus of power or the limitations of the popularity of the reforming cause.

42. K. Engelbert, "Die Anfänge der Lutherischen Bewegung in Breslau und Schlesien," *op. cit.*, p. 156: "ipsi autem domini pro majori hac [Martin Luther] heresi iam infecti erant."

43. W. Delius, *op. cit.*, p. 52. In 1531 ten (of seventeen) members of the Council did not receive Communion (*ibid.*, p. 48).

44. P. Roth, ed., *Aktensammlung zur Geschichte der Basler Reformation* (Basel, 1950), III, 291. Additional evidence from Basel includes a Protestant gathering involving between 300–500 burghers and another one with some 1,500—"der merteyl jung schrantzen, hantwergsgesellen und von den nechsten dörffern etliche buer": *Chronik des Fridelin Ryff, Basler Chroniken* (Leipzig, 1872), I, 57, 446.

45. P. Roth, *Die Reformation in Basel* (Basel, 1943), I, 48. An indirect bit of evidence for the sentiment among the Basel guilds is found in the Protestant de-

mand for the suppression of the Mass and the removal of the images; if this was not done by the Council, it should occur by voting of the guilds! (*ibid.*, II, 10).

46. B. Moeller, *op. cit., passim*.

47. L. v. Winterfeld, "Der Durchbruch der Reformation in Dortmund," *Beitr. z. Gesch. Dortmunds und der Grafschaft Mark*, 34 (1927), 57.

48. A. Zobel, "Untersuchungen über die Anfänge der Reformation in Görlitz und der Preussischen Oberlausitz," *Neues Lausitzisches Magazin*, 101 (1925), 158.

49. E. Egli, ed., *Actensammlung zur Geschichte der Zürcher Reformation in den Jahren 1519–1533* (Zurich, 1879), nos. 684, 1243.

50. E. Rohling, "Die Reichsstadt Memmingen in der Zeit der evangelischen Volksbewegung" (Diss., Munich, 1864), p. 43.

51. *Ratsbuch* 12, 110b, as quoted in A. Engelhardt, *Die Reformation in Nürnberg* (Nuremberg, 1936), I, 123. Other evidence of this sort may be cited—for example, in Breslau, where the St. Jacob's Church was overcrowded in 1523 on the occasion of Lutheran preaching (K. Engelbert, *op. cit.*, p. 172); also the demand of 150 burghers in Hildesheim to have Protestant preachers (K. Kayser, *Die Einführung der Reformation in der Stadt Hildesheim* [Hildesheim, 1883], p. 14). The same happened in Augsburg (Fr. Roth, *Augsburgs Reformationsgeschichte* [Munich, 1904], p. 117).

52. H. Haefliger, "Solothurn in der Reformation, 1519–1534," *op. cit.*, p. 40. My figures differ somewhat from those given by Haefliger, since I read the answers of the second survey differently. See also H. Haefliger, "Die solothurnische Volksanfragen vom Jahre 1529 über die konfessionelle Zuhörigkeit," *Jahrbuch f. Solothurnische Geschichte*, 11 (1938), 129–157. Voting also occurred (with one-sided results) in Lubeck (W. Jannasch, *op. cit.*, p. 275); Appenzell (J. Willi, *op. cit.*, p. 64), "man soll in jeglicher kirchhöri meeren, wellichen glouben sy wellti annemen."

53. As quoted in E. Naujoks, *Obrigkeitsgedanke, Zunftverfassung und Reformation* (Stuttgart, 1958), p. 74.

54. This consideration touches upon the question of motivation and commitment which shall occupy us at the end of our essay.

55. E. Naujoks, *op. cit.*, p. 88.

56. K. O. Muller, *Aktenstücke zur Geschichte der Reformation in Ravensburg* (Münster, 1914), p. 29, "ist darbei mit merer stimm beschlossen durch radt und gmaind, das man hinfüro das wort Gottes hie paur, lauter und rein verkünden und predigen solle."

57. See W. Jannasch, *Evangelischer Liederkrieg in Basel und Lübeck* (Munich, 1961), p. 17, "Dit singen makede en grot vorschreck aver de ganze stat." See also W. Jannasch, *Reformationsgeschichte Lübecks vom Petersablass bis zum Augsburger Reichstag 1515–1530* (Lubeck, 1958), p. 293. Singing was also a problem elsewhere: K. Kayser, *op. cit.*, pp. 10, 59.

58. P. Roth, *Durchbruch und Festsetzung der Reformation in Basel* (Basel, 1942), p. 18.

59. Whether there was a *Ratsreformation* has been contested; see B. Moeller, *op. cit.*, p. 61, and F. Lau, *op. cit.*, p. 119.

60. B. Moeller, *op. cit.*, pp. 62 ff.

61. The matter is complex. See Walton, "The Institutionalization of the Reformation at Zurich," *Zwingliana*, 13 (1972), 497–515; Muralt, "Stadtgemeinde und Reformation in der Schweiz," *Zeitschr. f. Schweiz. Gesch.*, 10 (1930), 349–384; Jacob, *Politische Führungsschicht und Reformation. Untersuchungen zur Reformation in Zürich 1519–1528* (Zurich, 1970).

62. In the case of Zurich the older thesis of N. Birnbaum, "The Zwinglian Reformation in Zurich," *Archives de Sociologie des Religions*, 8 (1959), 15–30,

which argued the appearance of a new ruling class, has been discounted by W. Jacob, *op. cit.*

63. Muller, *Die Wittenberger Bewegung 1521 und 1522* (Leipzig, 1911), p. 19. For Stralsund, see O. Plantiko, *Pommersche Reformationsgeschichte* (Greifswald, 1922), p. 31. For Basel, P. Roth, *Durchbruch und Festsetzung der Reformation in Basel*, p. 47. For Riga, Reval, Dorpat, L. Arbusow, *op. cit.*, pp. 290, 383. For Dortmund, L. v. Winterfeld, *op. cit.*, p. 63. For Kaufbeuren, K. Alt, *Reformation und Gegenreformation* (Munich, 1932), p. 17. For Memmingen, E. Rohling, *op. cit.*, p. 113. For Augsburg, F. Roth, *op. cit.*, pp. 130 ff. For Schaffhausen, J. Wipf, *op. cit.*, p. 154.

Ever since G. LeBon, *The Crowd: A Study of the Popular Mind* (New York, 1960), first published in 1896, social psychologists have paid attention to the psychology of mass movements. An extensive bibliography (as well as an excellent treatment) is found in O. E. Klapp, *Currents of Unrest: An Introduction to Collective Behavior* (New York, 1972), pp. 382–413. Historical studies, on the other hand, have been few; the best is G. Rudé, *The Crowd in History* (New York, 1964).

64. H. J. Hillerbrand, "The German Reformation and the Peasants' War," in L. P. Buck and J. Zophy, eds., *The Social History of the Reformation* (Columbus, 1972), pp. 106–136.

65. See the discussion of A. Friesen, *Reformation and Utopia: The Marxist Interpretation of the Reformation and Its Antecedents* (Wiesbaden, 1974).

66. K. Uhrig, "Der Bauer in der Publizistik der Reformation bis zum Ausgang des Bauernkrieges," *Archiv f. Reformationsgesch.*, 33 (1936), I: 70–125 and II: 165–225.

67. B. Moeller, *op. cit.*, p. 21.

68. A. G. Dickens, "Secular and Religious Motivation in the Pilgrimage of Grace," in G. J. Cuming, ed., *Studies in Church History*, IV (Leiden, 1967), 39–64.

69. L. v. Winterfeld, "Der Durchbruch der Reformation in Dortmund," *op. cit.*, p. 115, "dat hillighe Evangelium uth aldem unnd nyen Testamentt so vyll de predykantten dess uth goythlicker schrifftt bewern komnen." The town of Ansbach filed a formal grievance for the absence of "evangelical" preaching: K. Schornbaum, *Die Stellung des Markgrafen Kasimir von Brandenburg zur reformatorischen Bewegung in den Jahren 1524–1527* (Nuremberg, 1900), p. 242. In 1543 some fifty-seven burghers of Kempen appealed to Hermann von Wied "dass Ewr. Churfürstliche Gaaden uns doch mit einem sinceren Predicanden gnädiglich versehen . . . dass Gott . . . uns das Evangelum zu vergönnen," C. Krafft, "Briefe Melanchthons, Bucers und der Freunde und Gegner derselben," *Theol. Arbeiten* (Rhein. Wissenschaftl. Predigerverein) 2 (1874), 44. The same happened in Altenburg: A. Basedow, "Die Einführung der Reformation in Eisenberg," *Mitt. d. Gesch.- u. Altertumsforsch. Vereins z. Eisenberg*, 6 (1912), 181. See also W. Jannasch, *Reformationsgeschichte Lübecks vom Petersablass bis zum Augsburger Reichstag* (Lubeck, 1958), p. 275, "dat man gades wort to Lübeck predigen mochte."

70. In Lubeck, for example, the burghers made the authorization of Lutheran preachers the precondition for new tax levies: H. Schreiber, *Die Reformation Lübecks* (Halle, 1902), p. 45.

71. This point is made for Riga by L. Arbusow, *op. cit.*, p. 200.

72. Such local clerics as reformers are in evidence in Halle, for example, where a contemporary report has it that "der Dechant zu Halle sehr die Meinung D. Martini ausruft und dem Volk einbildet," as quoted in W. Delius, *op. cit.*, p. 26. In Leipzig 105 burghers submitted in 1524 a petition for a preacher of the "Word of God": Gotthard Lechler, "Die Vorgeschichte der Reformation Leipzigs," *Beitr.*

z. sächs. Kirchengesch., 3 (1885), 12. See also R. Dollinger, *Das Evangelium in Regensburg* (Regensburg, 1959), p. 135. F. A. Holzhausen, "Einführung der Reformation in . . . Goslar," *Histor. Vereins f. Niedersachsen Zeitschrift* (1851), XI, 337. In Constance the Lutheran preacher had "grossen zülouf vom gmainen volck," H.-Chr. Rublack, *Die Einführung der Reformation in Konstanz* (Gütersloh, 1971), p. 17. The same was said about Zwingli in Zurich; see O. Farner, *Huldrych Zwingli* (Zurich, 1954), III, 174. For Kitzingen see L. Michel, *Der Gang der Reformation in Franken* (Erlangen, 1930), p. 54; for Altdorf see L. Dirnhofer, "Die Reformation in Altdorf" (Diss., Erlangen, 1952), p. 46.

73. Heymann, "The Impact of Luther upon Bohemia," *Central European History,* 1 (1968), 107–130; Petri, "Mass und Bedeutung der reformatorischen Strömungen in den niederländischen Maaslanden im 16. Jahrhundert," in M. Greschat, ed., *Reformation und Humanismus* (Witten, 1969), pp. 212–234. D. M. Loades, "The Enforcement of Reaction, 1553–1558," *Journal of Eccl. History,* 16 (1965), 54, sees England at that time as neither Catholic nor Protestant, while A. G. Dickens, *Lollards and Protestants in the Diocese of York* (London, 1959), p. 214, finds that the immediate impact of official Protestanism upon the laity cannot be gauged. R. B. Manning, *op. cit.,* p. 48, asserts that "much more" needs to be known about popular Protestantism. Of contemporary sources we may note Erasmus' report (P. S. Allen, vol. III, no. 939) that Luther's books are read eagerly or Martin Bucer's note that the number of those professing the gospel is so great that their enemies begin to call the province [Normandy] "little Germany" (A.-L. Herminjard, ed., *Correspondance des Réformateurs dans les pays de langue française* [repr. Nieuwkoop, 1965], II, 271).

74. H. J. Hillerbrand, "The Spread of the Reformation of the Sixteenth Century," in C. D. Goodwin, ed., *The Transfer of Ideas* (Durham, N.C., 1968), pp. 80 ff.

75. A list of prohibited books, published on the Continent and smuggled into England in 1529, included some two dozen titles (in Latin, of course) from Luther; all in all, the list enumerated almost one hundred publications! G. S. Townsend and St. Cattley, eds., *The Acts and Monuments of John Foxe* (London, 1837), IV, 667 ff. C. S. Meyer, "Henry VIII Burns Luther's Books, 12 May, 1521" *op. cit.,* p. 178, records that one bookseller sold a dozen (!) of Luther's tracts. A careful bibliographical survey is given in R. Marius *et al.,* eds., *The Complete Works of St. Thomas More* (New Haven, 1973), VIII, 1063 ff.

76. It was, of course, one of the major emphases of the Reformation to appeal to the common people; see, for example, H. Junghans, "Der Laie als Richter im Glaubensstreit der Reformationszeit," *Luther-Jahrbuch,* 39 (1972), 31–54.

77. L. Febvre, "Une Question mal posée: Les Origines de la réforme française et le problème des causes de la réforme," *Au Coeur Religieux du XVIe Siècle* (Paris, 1970; orig. ed., 1957).

78. See, for example, *The Acts and Monuments of John Foxe* (London, 1838), V, 523–525: "The Story of a Poor Laboring Man."

79. G. Schramm, *op. cit.,* p. 56.

80. *Ibid.,* p. 55. Large Poland, with about one and one half million people, had some 120 Protestant congregations which, with the assumption of an average membership of 250 members, would suggest a total of 30,000 Protestants (*ibid.,* p. 27).

81. J. W. Thompson, *The Wars of Religion in France 1559–1576* (repr., New York, 1957), pp. 229 ff. Additional figures are cited there. Other statistical evidence comes from Alkmaar, where only some 160 burghers were Calvinists in 1576, out of a population of 6,000; see H. A. Enno van Gelder, *Revolutionaire reformatie* (Amsterdam, 1943), p. 20. In Amsterdam in 1585 the distribution of ecclesiastical

sentiment in the population was Catholics 51%, Lutherans 16%, and Calvinists and Anabaptists 32%; see R. Boumans, "De Getalsterkte van Katholieken en Protestanten 1585," *Revue Belge de Philologie et d'Histoire*, 30 (1952), 784.

82. L. Theobald, *Die Reformationsgeschichte der Reichsstadt Regensburg* (Munich, 1936), p. 130. Similar problems exist for other places, e.g., Erlangen: E. Dorn, *Die Reformation im ehemaligen Landstädtchen Erlangen* (Erlangen, 1929), p. 14.

IV

Problems in Editing Sixteenth- and Seventeenth-Century Letters

Giles E. Dawson
Former Curator of Books and Manuscripts
Folger Shakespeare Library

The subject of the brief discourse I am to deliver this afternoon, "Problems in Editing Sixteenth- and Seventeenth-Century Letters," may seem a bit narrow, but it ought to be stated even more narrowly as "English Letters Surviving in Manuscript." Actually, some of what I have to say will apply more broadly to the editing of any kind of sixteenth- and seventeenth-century manuscript and even to the editing of printed texts of that period.

The fundamental difference between printed text and manuscript text was suggested by a countryman who required help in the reading of a letter and excused his ignorance by saying, "I can read readin' but I can't read writin'." The problems that arise in the reading and transcribing of Renaissance texts are what I was invited to this Institute to help with, and they are among the problems that will concern us now.

The editorial standards that seemed good enough in the nineteenth century are not good enough now. The thin introductions, the meager annotation, and the slapdash texts provided by men like A. B. Grosart and Edward Arber served for the latter half of the last century.[1] More is required today, and new, well-edited texts are replacing the old, if not at a satisfactory pace. Of the collected letters of eminent writers of the past, recent decades have seen the production of those of Pope, Dr. Johnson, Walpole, George Eliot, and others. Robert Halsband, the editor of Lady Mary Wortley Montagu's letters,[2] has given us an admirable set of principles for the editing of eighteenth-century letters.[3]

But for letters of an earlier time, when the problems are rather different, no such statement of editorial principles has been undertaken. Nor, by and large, do adequate editions exist. If we would read letters written before 1650, we still have to rely mainly on such old-fashioned editors as Edmund Lodge, Sir Henry Ellis, and Logan Pearsall Smith.[4] Norman Davis's edition of the Paston Letters, now in progress, is an outstanding exception.[5]

The reasons for the comparative neglect of letters written in the sixteenth and the early seventeenth centuries are not hard to identify. Those whom Halsband calls *the* eighteenth-century letter-writers—Chesterfield, Lady Mary Wortley Montagu, and Walpole—can give pleasure to many readers outside the walls of academia, and so can men not primarily writers of letters, Johnson and Gray, for example. Before 1600 there were no letter-writers in Halsband's sense, only men and women who wrote letters. For the historian, Lord Burghley's hundreds of surviving letters are of great value, and they cry out to be gathered, edited, and printed. But no one bent on enjoyment alone can be expected to read a great many of them. Burghley had no time for small talk, and almost all of his letters are pure business.

Still, the sixteenth and seventeenth centuries are not barren of readable and enjoyable letters. Those of George Talbot, sixth Earl of Shrewsbury, to name one example, are loaded with human interest, especially those written during the years when he was chafing under the burden of keeping the Queen of Scots, and under the miseries arising from his reckless marriage to the infamous Bess of Hardwick. The letters that survive from the sixteenth and seventeenth centuries are mainly those of the gentry and the nobility, and these wrote to one another only when they had something important to communicate. Dispatching a letter involved dispatching a servant to carry it.

What Halsband provided for letter-writers of the eighteenth century it is my purpose now to offer for those of the sixteenth and seventeenth. I can best accomplish this by using as my point of reference not the letters of one man or one woman, but the correspondence of a family that happens to blanket neatly the reigns of Queen Elizabeth and James I.

The correspondence is now in the Folger Shakespeare Library, and the family is the Bagot family. The Bagots were firmly settled in Staffordshire in the middle of the twelfth century and by the middle of the sixteenth century were among the most influential families in the southern half of the county. What remains of their correspondence is more than a thousand letters and fifty or sixty supporting documents—the correspondence of two successive heads of the family—Richard, who died in 1597, and Walter, who died in 1623.

Richard typified the old, established gentry, secure in his position, well endowed with land, consanguine with many of the best families. But he appears to have enjoyed a rather special reputation, and he worked hard to maintain it. He was well known and well trusted, not only by his neighbors but by the Privy Council and the Queen herself. He was a justice of the peace, and a very active one. He was also, under the Lord Lieutenant Shrewsbury, one of the deputy lieutenants of his county, and it says something about Bagot that, after one of his two fellow deputies died and the other resigned, he was left to discharge alone the sensitive and burdensome duties of the office. He was in addition twice sheriff, a commissioner for recusants, steward of crown lands in Staffordshire, and the Queen's woodward.

These jobs kept him busy, and they generated a major part of the correspondence. There are in the collection, for example, fifty-four letters from the Privy Council, forty from Lord Treasurer Burghley, some sixty from Shrewsbury, a score from the Earls of Essex and Lords Paget and Stafford, and many from minor officials of church and state. From these letters emerges a man of outstanding tact as well as energy, who could faithfully execute his duties as commissioner of recusants without generating ill feeling among the recusant gentry of a county believed in some quarters to be a hotbed of Catholicism. He could deliver the goods when Essex demanded one of the county seats in Parliament for his stepfather, and he could give the Earl a rebuff when he asked for the second seat. He could defend himself with dignity against an unreasonable tantrum of Shrewsbury's or an arrogant and bad-mannered attack by Lord Stafford. In none of these incidents do Bagot's warm relations with the great men involved appear to suffer.

Bagot was clearly a hard-working man, and the work was taxing. But it paid off in the coin that Bagot would have valued most highly—connections. He was able to marry Walter, his heir, to a niece of Lord Burghley (a connection that in turn stood Walter in good stead all the rest of his life). For his other son, Anthony, he obtained a position with the twelve-year-old Essex that lasted until the fall of the Earl, who had by that time provided a good marriage for Anthony. Of Richard's daughters one was married to a gentleman lawyer who later became a judge. Two other daughters got heirs to desirable estates.

Richard's successor, Walter, was somewhat less active in public affairs, but he is a more interesting correspondent than his father because of the better survival of his copies of his own letters as compared with the survival of Richard's copies of his, and because he had family problems—a recalcitrant eldest son, a sister with great troubles, and another sister early widowed. Also he was called upon more often than his father was by neighbors who needed help or sympathy.

When these letters came to the Folger Shakespeare Library in 1955, I was soon impressed with the wealth of publishable material that they contained. I resolved that when time permitted I would tackle the job of making some of the letters available in print. The time is available, and I have tackled it. The first major question that faced me was whether I ought to publish the entire correspondence, and the answer that eventually emerged was negative. To start with, the 1,048 letters, properly edited, would fill three or four thousand pages, three or four big and expensive volumes, and I doubt that any press would touch it. Pope, Johnson, Walpole, Voltaire, Franklin, Adams, Jefferson, yes. But who ever heard of the Bagots, apart from that Bagot who associates with Bushy and Green in Shakespeare's

Richard II? Furthermore, it would be unwise to publish fifty Privy Council letters only because they happen to have been sent to one man. Nor would it be wise to print forty of Burghley's letters or sixty of the Earl of Shrewsbury's or a dozen of Essex's, because this would reduce the likelihood that someone might want to publish the collected letters of these men. Finally, a fair number of the Bagot letters are wholly unintelligible because the subject matter was so familiar to both writer and addressee that explanation was unneeded. In the collected letters of one man everything must be included, but in such a mixed lot as the Bagot correspondence no such necessity exists. Stripped, then, of the Privy Council letters and the others that I have mentioned, the rest of the collection would make a formless assemblage of loosely related letters. I therefore concluded that the best way to proceed would be to print groups of letters which in some essential way are related.

Having decided what to publish, one next faces the question of what kind of text to provide. At one extreme is the text that approaches facsimile reproduction as closely as is possible in print—retaining the original spelling, capital letters, and all contractions and abbreviations. This is the kind of text in which the Malone Society prints old plays and dramatic records from manuscript. It offers the advantage of putting all the evidence clearly before the reader and letting him determine the meanings intended by a writer. For the editor there remains only the responsibility of accurate transcription. The result suits the needs of the Malone Society admirably. But for other textual purposes the advantage inherent in such a text is at least partly offset by two disadvantages. The first of these, that an old-spelling text slows the reader down, does not much impress me. The second is more serious. What the type-facsimile text slows down is both composition and proofreading in the printing house, and this adds substantially to costs—which today seem exorbitant at best—so substantially that it may in some cases be the deciding factor in a publisher's decision to accept or reject a work.

At the other extreme is the text in which the usages of our

own time in spelling, punctuation, capitals, and so forth are adopted. While this method will satisfy the reader who has no concern with language and cares only for content, it is beset with pitfalls. Where does one draw the line in modernizing text? When the Folger Library initiated a new series of reprints some twelve years ago, the first volume consisted of unpublished writings of William Lambarde, edited by the late Conyers Read,[6] and to me fell the task of reforming Read's transcribed text. I have great respect for Conyers Read as an historian. But being a good historian does not in itself make a man a good editor. For the Lambarde book he provided a necessary and valuable introduction, but he was wanting in the patience if not in the knowledge required for the performance of what Alexander Pope called the dull duties of an editor, and I came to suspect that Read did not know what the duties were. He failed to exhibit the requisite zeal in wrestling with the difficult handwriting of Lambarde's rough drafts, in which interlines are not infrequently written over interlines. And Read had a tendency, worse still, to modernize everything, including grammar, and was not above substituting a different word now and then for an archaism he thought the average reader would not understand. Such abhorrent standards are not characteristic of historians in general.

The choice does not lie solely between the Malone Society's kind of text and Read's kind. There are acceptable compromises, of which the first is to retain the writer's spelling, punctuation, and capital letters but bring down all raised letters and expand all contractions, either with or without italics for the expansions. This is Halsband's way with Lady Mary Wortley Montagu, and I have no quarrel with it for texts of the eighteenth century, in which spelling variants are too few to affect the printing speed seriously. The other compromise modernizes spelling, punctuation, capital letters, and of course contractions. This is the kind of text I prefer.

What, after all, is gained by reproducing a letter-writer's spelling? If a non-standard spelling communicates a meaning, the standard spelling will communicate the same meaning, not different or less. Sixteenth-century readers surely paid no attention to spelling so long as they readily grasped what was meant, but curious spellings could, even for them, obscure meaning. A lady writing to Walter Bagot wanted to refer to him as one of three feoffees, but instead of "feoffees" wrote "feth feth." The context does not make the meaning at once obvious, and Bagot may have had some trouble with it, though probably less than I experienced. Would anyone recommend that in printing this letter the editor ought to retain "feth feth" and supply "feoffees" in a footnote? Another point to be considered is that old spelling imparts to a text a spurious quaintness, a quality that the writer did not intend. There are proper uses for old spelling— in textual studies, for example. But I am inclined to feel that those who urge it for all purposes are intent upon promoting the mystique of scholarship.

There is more to be said for the use of old spelling in the printing of manuscript material, where the spelling may be that of the writer, than in the reprinting of printed matter, where the spelling will almost certainly be that of the compositor, not of the writer. But it must be borne in mind that in the sixteenth century many gentlemen and most noblemen employed clerks to copy their rough drafts.

When an editor does choose to print old-spelling text (whether of a letter or other matter, whether from manuscript copy or printed), he is obliged also to reproduce the original punctuation and, I incline to think (disagreeing here with Halsband), even capital letters. The retention of the old spelling creates a presumption that the other accidentals are likewise retained. Any departure from the original must then be noted. Both Arber and Grosart print old spelling but occasionally (and only occasionally) alter punctuation and regularly expand contractions—all silently. And I suspect old Lodge of doing the same thing, though his instincts led him to perform some of the duties of an editor better than most of his nineteenth-century successors did.

Whatever textual practices an editor employs, he must provide a full and detailed statement of them in his introduction. No editor that I know of performed this duty fully before 1900.

The editor must, of course, be scrupulous to preserve the language and the grammar of his text—even bad sentence structure, unless it obscures meaning, and if it does that and if re-punctuation cannot cure the fault, bracketed elements may be inserted to make the meaning clear. His scrupulous care in preservation of the language ought also to extend to the inclusion of archaic word forms as distinct from spellings. I mean words like "sithens" for "since," "fet" for "fetched," "band" for "bond," "abouts" for "about," and such dialectic forms as "yealth" for "health" and "knowen" for "known." One of Richard Bagot's sons-in-law habitually wrote that word "kenown" and doubtless so pronounced it, and it ought to be retained. It is a gross error for an editor to obliterate the individuality of a writer's speech or to modernize Elizabethan language.

It is characteristic of handwriting that each hand is unique and that hands vary in quality and legibility. It will always be probable, therefore, that the transcriber of any hand but those written with the greatest care will come upon letters, words, or larger elements that, try as he may, he simply cannot make out with any certainty. The commonest cause of this difficulty is, of course, bad writing due to haste, carelessness, or sloppy habits. Most commonly such problems can be solved. By diligently poring over a page or two of a bad hand, taking careful note of the writer's letter forms and linkages and paying special attention to what is eccentric in the hand, the transcriber usually may remove all difficulties. This does not necessarily mean that he can read every individual letter. He may discover that his writer habitually reduces final -*ing*, for example, to a short horizontal line with a downstroke at the end. The transcriber in these cases cannot actually read the letters because they are not there, but he can accurately read the writer's intention, and that is all that can be expected. In a very badly written hand even this may prove impossible. Queen Elizabeth, whose writing-master is said to have been Roger Ascham, wrote a beautiful signature and on occasion a whole beautiful letter. But when she dashed off a brief and private letter—some of which have survived—the writing was abominably and almost uniformly illegible. With hard work one can make out most of the sense of her message but sometimes not all of the words. In such cases the transcriber must resort to guessing or must simply give up, and in either event he must furnish a note describing the difficulty and the nature of his solution, if he has reached one.

Rather easier to deal with, at least less costly in time, are lacunae and omissions. Lacunae resulting from damp decay may be extensive or may affect the ends of many lines. Here restoration is hardly to be attempted, and all the transcriber can do is indicate the nature and extent of the loss. Where damage results from ink blots, perforations, or tears, and affects only a word or two, restoration within square or angled brackets is in order if the context encourages it. All such restorations require appropriate notes. So, of course, does the insertion of a word, if it is a substantive word omitted through the writer's carelessness. A simple and obvious word like "did," "has," or "was," presumed to be omitted through carelessness, may be inserted in brackets without a note. An accidental reduplication of a word may in good conscience, it seems to me, be omitted silently, the writer's intention being the governing consideration. As to a deletion by the writer, we can easily imagine situations in which the deleted matter, if legible, would be worthy of preservation. In the rough draft of a poem, for example, any deletion and substitution would almost certainly warrant preservation. In a letter, unless style and diction are important considerations, nothing would be gained by recording the deletion. The editor ought to feel free to decide the question in accordance with the needs of the text.

In short I am opposed to mere finickiness. No one would want an editor to supply a note for every unreadable or questionable letter. If a word is in question—particularly a word of some importance—it needs a note. What the editor is bound to preserve is the writer's thought clothed in the writer's own language, not his commas, his spellings, and his trifling mistakes.

An example of finickiness of another sort—of paying attention to trifling details while neglecting basic editorial responsibilities—is to be found in a thin work called *Shakespeare's Love's Labor's Won* (Carbondale, Ill., 1957), edited by the late Professor T. W. Baldwin. He tells of finding a folio volume in a seventeenth-century binding in which two sheets of manuscript had been folded and sewn in to strengthen the sewing of the first and last gatherings of the book—a not uncommon practice of the time. Baldwin tells of taking the book to a skillful handbinder who removed the old threads and marked them so that they could be carefully preserved with the manuscript sheets, one thread from the front sheet, one from the back, as if they were sacred relics. The manuscript proved to be from the accounts of an obscure Jacobean bookseller, including an inventory of books in stock, among which was a play called "loves labor lost" and another called "loves labor won." Francis Meres had included these two plays in a list less than ten years earlier as by William Shakespeare. Baldwin furnishes reproductions of the three manuscript pages, with facing transcripts, among which, I am sorry to say, are at least twenty mistakes, big and little, in transcription. Had he exhibited the same reverence for the text that he showed for the sewing thread, his book would have been better than it is.

When Pope spoke of the dull duties of an editor, he must have had in mind the collating of earlier editions, which, to his credit, he knew to be important though he had done very little of it. In comparison with a Shakespeare text, especially as it must now be reconstructed under the rigorous discipline developed by McKerrow, Greg, and Bowers, the text of letters printed from manuscript presents few problems.

When we come to the annotation, as we must now do, the challenging part of the work begins. By way of making the consideration of this function as concrete as possible I am going to present three letters, which will serve as laboratory specimens. The first is from Sir Thomas Cokayne to Richard Bagot.

Right worshipful and my old good friend, I have now just occasion to prove your friendship. I am given to understand that Mr. Okeover and his man Parker, either the one or both, contrary to their oaths, go about to procure a privy sessions against my son, who, playing a young man's part as it should seem, went about to take away his daughter and yet failed thereof and was procured by the gentlewoman so to do. I trust to have your especial friendship herein, praying you to advertise me of the day and pl[ace] of your sitting. Thus with my hearty commendations to you and good Mrs. Bagot with all your children, I commit you to God's almighty protection. Ashbourne, this 28th of May 1579.

Yours as his own,
Thomas Cokayne

A letter of this nature ought usually to be preceded or followed, in an edition, by an extended commentary in addition to such brief textual and glossarial notes as are required. The commentary to this letter must identify Cokayne as a Derbyshire man who was born in 1519 and died in 1592, grew up in the household of George, Earl of Shrewsbury, came into a large inheritance in 1538, and was the author of a book called *A Short Treatise of Hunting* (1591).[7] If at first glance there is some apparent ambiguity as to whose daughter was involved, it vanishes when we note that she is called "gentlewoman" and therefore cannot be the daughter of Master Okeover's "man Parker," obviously no gentleman. The kidnapping failed, but the young man must have done more than go about or prepare to take the girl away, for that would not have been an actionable offense. Of the statement that he "was procured by the gentlewoman so to do" I can make nothing beyond the obvious suggestion that the lady was at least willing. Whether or not the prosecution took place we cannot know, because the 1579 records of the Privy Sessions at Stafford are not extant. Sir Thomas's assumption that Bagot would be one of the justices sitting in the next Privy Sessions suggests his knowledge that Bagot was, of the twenty-two Staffordshire justices of the peace, one of the most faithful in his discharge of this duty. Finally, it must be pointed out that Cokayne's eldest son, Thomas, and Mr. Okeover's only daughter and presumptive heiress, Jane, were married not long after the incident.

Here I believe I supply all the identifications and all the information that the reader of this letter would require, and I avoid going beyond that requirement, giving more information than is called for—a not uncommon vice in editors. George Eland, editor of the Shardeloes Papers, put out in 1960 a little volume of letters by Sir Thomas Wotton, a Kentishman and father of Sir Henry.[8] But assuredly Sir Henry, a celebrated letter-writer, did not learn the art at his father's knee. Sir Thomas's letters are uniformly dull. It may have been recognition of this fact, and of the additional fact that his volume was going to be a thin one, that led Eland to alleviate both deficiencies with voluminous notes. That these contain valuable information and make good reading does not justify him, for many of the notes go far beyond the needs of the letters. He would have been well advised to forget about the letters altogether and give himself over to unadulterated local history of Kent.

The Cokayne letter requires no footnotes. The brackets employed in the word "place" contain missing letters so obvious as to need no further explanation. The word "commendations" in the complimentary close of the letter has, in the manuscript, lost the last six letters, but the word is so conventional, so ubiquitous, and so unvarying in this context in letters of the time as to leave no doubt whatever of the correct reading here and to obviate even the need of brackets. To use them would be merely finicky.

But let us pursue a little further the career of Jane Okeover, who has now become Lady Ashley and is perhaps twenty years older than she was when Tom Cokayne tried to elope with her. Here is her first letter to Walter Bagot:

Good Cousin, the good conceit I have of you, and in that my father's house and yours is linked together in so sure a bond of amity, I thought I could not make choice of any so well as yourself, both in regard of the Christian love I hope you bear me as also for your wisdom and good conscience. It hath pleased my father to make a lease to my use and to beset me five hundred pound in money, the which is to be delivered to three feoffees in trust, [of] the which yourself is one, my uncle Okeover the other, and Mr. Egerton of Ridley the third. The lease is under the value of thirty pound by the year; it is for twenty-one years if I live so long. I was not desirous to have anything to the hindrance of my name or house; but in that the indenture had the relation of a lease I would not a desired it. It behoveth me to have it kept in great secretsy, and I doubt not of your care herein, for if it should be known to my husband it may work me more grief than the thing is like to benefit me, by reason it is unperfect, for unless my uncle and yourself can persuade my father to make a will and give a true copy unto every of the feoffee[s'] hand[s], whereby you may recover the five hundred pound at my father's decease, it is to no end. I pray you let me be so much beholden to you as to come to Okeover to set your hand to the indenture before my going to London. And so with friendly commendation to you, desiring you to read and burn, I commit you to God.

> She that makes account of you
> as one of her best friends,
> Jane A.

When Jane wrote this letter her first husband was dead and she was married to Sir Anthony Ashley, previously secretary to the Privy Council, and they had a daughter, Anne, who, after marrying Sir John Cooper, became the mother of Dryden's Achitophel, the first Earl of Shaftsbury. Jane's father, Philip Okeover, was possessed of seven or eight manors in Staffordshire and Derbyshire, and Jane was a thumping big heiress. It must have been before 1590 that Ashley married her, for in that year she ceased to be an heiress when her father executed a conveyance of the family estates to his brother Rowland upon his (Philip's) death. Rowland had a son, Ralph, who in 1587 had taken to wife Dorothy, Walter Bagot's sister—a relationship that explains why Jane, with characteristic Elizabethan license, starts her letter, "Good Cousin." It may be imagined that Sir Anthony was annoyed when he learned that his wife was not the heiress that he had been led to believe she was, and he straightaway instituted litigation aimed at getting the conveyance to Rowland annulled. He even tried to persuade the Queen to interfere to that end. But if she did so it was ineffectual, for the property passed smoothly to Rowland upon his brother's death in 1604. Meanwhile Rowland's son, Walter Bagot's brother-in-law, had died childless, and in view of this, Rowland, aged seventy and more, unwilling to remain without an heir, married, and in due course his wife made things right. I might add, to complete the story, that the child, soon orphaned, became Bagot's ward and was married to one of his daughters while both were infants.

At the time of the writing of this letter Jane's father was obviously alive and had drawn an instrument—that feoffment which leased property for a term of years to three feoffees (Jane in her ignorance called them "feth feth"), of whom Walter Bagot was one and Jane's uncle, the heir, was another. The purpose of the lease was to provide an income for the disinherited Jane, and it was in the form of a feoffment designed to limit the lease to her sole use in order to entrust the property into the hands of three trustworthy men who would protect her interests. Such were the nature and the purpose of feoffments.

The date of the letter cannot be established closely. That it was written after 1597, when Richard Bagot died and the family estates passed to Walter, is shown by the address of the letter to Walter Bagot "at his house at Blithfield." And it was written before Jane's father died in 1604.

It may be complained that I have committed the very fault with which I charged George Eland. The commentary is long, indeed. But in an edition of a group of Bagot letters anything that establishes a relationship between the Bagot family and the writers of the letters is legitimate. On the other hand, perhaps the connection with Dryden's Achitophel is superfluous.

We still need three footnotes—the first to point out that Jane wrote "feth feth" instead of "feoffees," the second to define "beset" as to give or bestow, and the third to identify the third feoffee, Mr. Egerton of Ridley, as Ralph Egerton, whose seat in Cheshire was close enough to the Okeover seat, Okeover, to qualify him as a near neighbor.

And now one more letter from Jane, Lady Ashley, a sequel to the first.

Cousin Bagot, it is thought good that you and the rest of the feoffees should i-write to my Lord Chancellor to let him understand of such a lease made to yourself and the rest so long sithens, in regard that Mr. Ashley hath not given me any maintenance for five or six years, and to entreat his lordship that the said lease may stand in the same manner and form as it was intended by my father, using the same words that are in the lease, desiring you to send me a true copy of the lease of Haywood, and I will cause Mr. Baxter to dray a letter in your names to my Lord Chancellor and will send it you to set your hand to hit. And so, hoping to hear from you, I commit you to God, with my kind commendations to you and your wife.

Your poor cousin,
Jane Ashley

My own want will drive me to complain. I must not have all taken from me and set content with nothing but words, for his promises are like the wind. Worse than I am I cannot be. If my Lord Chancellor will not right me the Council will, I hope. I know one that is inward with the king. I will not be so ruined, God willing. I will sell the gown to my back before. What is he that men should fear him, whose breath is in nostrils? God that brought Nebuchadnezzar's pride to nought can humble him, I doubt not.

In letters perhaps more than in other kinds of writing there will be obscure matters that the editor cannot explain. But is it needful that he constantly proclaim his inability to make this point or that clear? It will often happen that a point can be elucidated from another letter in the collection or from an external source. Thus in annotating Sir Thomas Cokayne's letter I was able to say that young Cokayne in due course married Jane Okeover. But if I had had no such information and had said nothing further about the affair, the reader would assume that nothing further was known about it.

So in this second letter of Jane Ashley's there is no need to speculate about the nature of the Lord Chancellor's involvement in her difficulties. That the first lease here mentioned is the same discussed in the previous letter appears nearly certain, and it is unnecessary to say so. Nor is there any necessity to express my ignorance of the identity of the man who, in Jane's splendid postscript, is "inward with the king." My lack of information on this will readily be assumed. That the "lease of Haywood" is not the lease mentioned earlier and that I have no information about it might well be pointed out. That Mr. Baxter is unidentified does need to be pointed out, as well as the fact that Jane wrote "Mr. Bacter" and that "Baxter" is my emendation. The main puzzle is "Mr. Ashley." Sir Anthony was knighted in 1596, before the writing of Jane's first letter, and it is inconceivable that she should demote him to plain Mr. Ashley. Elizabethans were not casual about titles. I am inclined to speculate that Sir Anthony's father, perhaps having her dowry in his hands, had earlier felt himself obliged to make subsistence payments to her. Of small footnotes, two are needed—one to explain that "dray" is a northern dialect form of "draw," another to identify "whose breath is in nostrils" in Jane's postscript as lifted from Isaiah 2:22.

The date of the letter is yet to be dealt with, and there is little evidence to go on. We found Jane's first letter to be no earlier than November, 1597, and now the drawing of the lease, then recent, is "long sithens," and King James is on the throne. Any speculation about a specific year would be blind guessing.

And finally, as a postscript of my own, I should like to add that the Bagot collection is rich in publishable material, and that it is available. I have nearly ready for publication a group of twenty-four letters written by two generations of Bagot sons when they were students at Oxford, and I am at work on another group of letters concerned with marriage. But I should be loth to leave the impression that I have any sort of claim to the rest of the collection. I particularly hope to interest someone in the forty-odd letters by Richard Bagot's son-in-law Richard Broughton, a man of law, an agent to the young Earl of Essex, a member of Parliament, and a judge in Wales. It would be a rewarding task, and there are others.

Notes

1. To both of these men generations of students have been deeply indebted for the flood of sixteenth- and seventeenth-century reprints that they produced between 1868 and 1900. Many of these, mostly of minor works, are still readily available in no other shape. Arber's fifty-four volumes contain more than fifty whole books and hundreds of ephemera. Most of them are in old spelling, reproduced with a fair degree of accuracy. His introductions, usually of no more than half a dozen pages, are hasty compilations, mainly biographical and bibliographical. His annotations are, when not entirely wanting, sparse and inadequate. Our greatest single debt to Arber is, of course, for his transcripts of the Stationers' Register. Grosart's output was, in its bulk, four or five times that of Arber. It embraces a great number of small and obscure works besides the collected works of Spenser, Greene, and Daniel, and Dekker's prose works. His introductions are much more substantial than Arber's but now of small value, his notes more numerous but still inadequate. His old-spelling texts are less reliable than Arber's. Both men tamper with the punctuation and silently expand contractions—practices inconsistent with the pseudo-facsimile appearance imparted by the use of tall esses and of Elizabethan *u* and *v*, *i* and *j*.

2. *The Complete Letters of Lady Mary Wortley Montagu*, 3 vols. (Oxford, 1965–1967).

3. "Editing the Letters of Letter-Writers," *Studies in Bibliography*, 11 (1958), 25–37.

4. Lodge's *Illustrations of British History, Biography, and Manners, in the Reigns of Henry VIII, Edward VI, Mary, Elizabeth, and James I* (London, 1791; reprinted 1838) contains selections of the correspondence of the fifth and sixth earls of Shrewsbury said to be from a fifteen-volume collection of Shrewsbury correspondence in the College of Arms (where Lodge was successively Norroy and Clarenceux King-of-Arms), together with selected correspondence of several dukes of Norfolk and of Lord Burghley. Lodge ostensibly reproduces the old spelling and contractions but tells us nothing further about his editorial practices. He provides a meager introduction and reasonably abundant annotation. Sir Henry Ellis's principal collection of letters is *Original Letters, Illustrative of English History*, in three series totaling eleven volumes, 1824 to 1846. The letters are of the fifteenth to the eighteenth centuries. There are no introductions, but Ellis supplies headnotes to some letters and a few footnotes. His *Original Letters of Eminent Literary Men*, Camden Soc., vol. XXIII (London, 1843), extend from 1550 to 1799. Again there are no introductions and only sparse notes. All the letters in both Ellis's collections are ostensibly in old spelling, but he is silent about his editorial practices. Logan Pearsall Smith, in *The Life and Letters of Sir Henry Wotton* (two volumes, Oxford, 1907), displays an admirable grasp of the duties of an editor. His text is, for so early a date, surprisingly good, and his documentation errs only in being less generous than one might wish. Smith's exposition of his editorial principles consists mainly of a statement of his reasons for adopting modern spelling—the right reasons.

5. *Paston Letters and Papers of the Fifteenth Century*, volume I of three projected volumes (Oxford, 1971).

6. *William Lambarde and Local Government* (Ithaca, N. Y., 1962).

7. *STC* 5457.

8. *Thomas Wotton's Letter-Book, 1574–1586* (London, 1960).

V

Vital and Artistic Structures in the Life of Don Quixote

Juan Bautista Avalle-Arce
University of North Carolina at Chapel Hill

Man was created in God's image, and he has never quite forgotten it. Even in his more rabid moments of atheism, man is not so much concerned with the denial of God as with the issue of placing himself in God's stead. Man has always needed models for his actions and aspirations, if only, for no better reason, to use those models as excuses or scapegoats. History shows it to be painfully evident that the cloak of emulation has always covered equally well both vices and virtues, famous accomplishments and infamous misdeeds.

In this respect literature has been both used and abused by man. The proper use of literature, within my present context, lies mainly in the general area of inspirational works. Its abuse comes about when the imitation of literature is seen as an end in itself, without any evidently redeeming transcendence of purpose. I will readily grant you that the dividing line between use and abuse is thin and thorny, because it so happens that most of us do lead a centaur-like existence in which we crossbreed fact and fiction, reality and imagination. We all know that Walter Mitty was wrong, but do we all know, equally well, *where* he went wrong?

I propose to talk to you today about the archetype of all the Walter Mittys of this world, a man who made a creed of imagination, a rationale of fiction; a man whose life was embodied in the first and greatest modern novel. I propose to talk to you about how Don Quixote brought his life to the level of art, disdaining to acknowledge humdrum reality, and how in allowing him to do so his creator exposed forever those tenuous and delicate links which create, almost paradoxically, that inextricable mixture of fact and fancy which is life.

The very beginning of the novel is clearly indicative of the new system of coordinates that Cervantes postulates between life and literature. Everyone remembers the classic opening: "In a certain village in La Mancha, which I do not wish to name, there lived not long ago a gentleman . . . ," and the rest of the description, which must be in everybody's mind.[1] The richness of detail of the portrait, with its accumulation of beef-stew, lentils, slippers, etc., practically makes us lose sight of one most important fact: what the author gives us so glibly is everything that is external to the gentleman in question. Those accumulated details are totally adjectival. They say nothing of the substance of the man. The details trace the outline of a man about whom, basically, we know next to nothing.

To start with, the author willfully avoids giving us the name of his hero's birthplace, and one is to remember that geography has always been credited with a strong determinism on the human being. Without pretending at all to go into science or pseudo-science, we just have to remember that the late George Apley would be completely inconceivable as anything but a proper Bostonian, and that the protagonists of William Faulkner's novels would be total misfits in any place other than their fictional South. Obviously, at least in literature, birthplace has been understood as a means of determining conduct.

In the second place, Cervantes refuses to give his protagonist a name. As he puts it, "They say that his surname was Quixada or Quesada—for there is some difference of opinion amongst authors on this point. However, by very reasonable conjecture we may take it that he was called Quexana." And at the end of the book the protagonist is not called by any of these three possibilities, but rather by a fourth one: Quixano. Now, in the Judaeo-Christian tradition personal names have always been conceived as having a certain mystical quality of capturing some aspect of the essence of that person. That is why changes in names often have been so important in the lives of individuals.

No one can confuse Saul of Tarsus and Saint Paul, or Jacob and Israel, yet they are one and the same person. An essential change in personality, and its new, vital orientation, are expressed by a change in name. This is parallelled, and very purposefully, in *Don Quixote*, where the protagonist is called by a variety of names after he has invented his own and christened himself Knight of the Sad Countenance, Knight of the Lions, etc. But I cannot go into that here.

The point I want to make now, apropos of names, is twofold: one, a person's name was believed to have a certain definitory quality; two, our protagonist is a gentleman without a name. This last is quite extraordinary. It is a complete contradiction in terms, since the first quality of nobility is lineage, that is to say, the history of the family name. In other words, our protagonist is presented to us without the age-old determinism of blood, family, and traditions.

The novels written prior to Cervantes, most particularly the chivalresque and the picaresque novels, were built squarely on precisely that type of determinism. Their protagonists were the way they were because birthplace, name, family, blood, and tradition weighed so heavily on them that they could not be otherwise. Take the first Spanish chivalresque novel, *Amadís de Gaula*: the protagonist is the son of a beautiful princess and of the King of Gaul, and grandson of the King of Britain. Hence he will grow up to be the most perfect hero. Or take the protagonist of the first Spanish picaresque novel, the *Lazarillo de Tormes*: he is born near Salamanca, the son of a thieving miller and of a woman who goes to live with a Negro slave after the death of her husband. It is easy to see that the child is predetermined to become a most accomplished scoundrel.

If you will notice now, it is precisely their heritage which determined that Amadís or Lazarillo would develop one way or another, and it is precisely a heritage that is absent in the case of Don Quixote. Our hero stands out, by comparison, like a new Adam, unattached to anything prior to him, with no past to lay claims on him, with no name, even, which could somehow fix some part of his personality. The literary implications of this innovation are prodigious. In the traditional novels the life of the protagonist is seen as a predetermined capsule which travels at a measured speed through time and space, with little control on the part of the rider, to a preassigned destination. In the novel of Cervantes, however, life is essentially a pattern of choices, continuous and sometimes agonizing choices among possibilities. That is why the figure of the protagonist has been carefully trimmed of all those characteristics which could have hindered his free choice. Whatever possibilities life may open to him are his to choose from freely, untrammelled by geographical factors, name, family, etc.

When we consider the matter closely, we see that the protagonist has at least a triple choice as the novel opens: one, he can keep on being a country squire, with all the attending excitements of eating partridge every Sunday; two, he can become a writer, a possibility hinted at when we are told that occasionally, in his madness, he has thought of putting pen to paper and writing a few chivalresque adventures of his own; and three, he can become a knight-errant. That he chooses the last of these, the most incredible of all the options, is to me the best argument that the new literary character has the most complete freedom of choice.

I do not want to finish this part of my exposition without bringing to your attention a delightful irony of Cervantes. He tells us that it was after his protagonist lost his mind, and only then, that he decided to become a knight-errant and thus, figuratively, to "write" chivalresque adventures. But this is what Cervantes himself was doing at that very same moment. So we are led inescapably to conclude that Cervantes is as crazy as his protagonist. This is an irony, but it is no joke. To me it is very serious, because I look upon it as the most delicately effective way that Cervantes could create an almost divine proportion of likeness between creator and creature. This likeness liberates and dignifies the literary creature. And the acquisition of dignity implies the acquisition of the will necessary to be oneself and not anyone else. That is to say, it implies the sure and firm vital option.

So the protagonist chooses, firmly and surely, and what he decides is to be Don Quixote de la Mancha, a knight-errant. His mind is full of models, which he decides to imitate so as to bring his life as close as he can to the perfection possible within his chosen destiny. In short, from the moment of his self-baptism Don Quixote decides to make of life a work of art. The world he aspires to live in is a world of art, and, therefore, everything in humdrum reality has to be transmuted into its artistic equivalent if it is to have a place. Hence his horse, which can no longer remain in blissful but unpoetic anonymity, is dragged into the full light of art (and of strife) under the sonorous name of "Rocinante."

As early, at least, as Plato's *Protagoras*, man entertained the notion that by imitating art he assured his life a new dimension, which has, at various times, been called by such names as wisdom, virtue, or fame. By the time of the Renaissance this principle of the imitation of models acquired a new dimension, because by then it was art itself which must imitate art. Or as Giorgio Vasari put it in the preface to his *Lives of the Painters*: "Our art consists entirely of imitation, first of Nature, and then, as it cannot rise so high of itself, of those things which are produced from the masters with the greatest reputation."

But the old idea that life should imitate art and thereby somehow become a work of art by itself was still very much there. This was quite natural in a time which Jacob Burckhardt has characterized, in his classic book on *The Civilization of the Renaissance in Italy*, as the age which developed the concept of the state as a work of art. Charles V, the great emperor, the first and only emperor of the Old World and the New, was a firm believer and practitioner of the concept of life as a work of art. In trying to synthesize in his life and in his politics the contradiction between medieval aspirations and modern possibilities, Charles was incarnating the very essence of the Renaissance ideal of world harmony. He was striving for the noblest form of life as a work of art.

I mention these facts only in passing, so as to provide a brief backdrop to the ideals and actions of our knight from La Mancha. Don Quixote's practice of the principle of imitating models, and his efforts to make his life into a work of art fall in line with both the vital attitudes of Charles V and the aesthetic pronouncements of Giorgio Vasari. To be sure, Don Quixote has problems in implementing his ideal, problems which have little in common with international politics or aesthetics. Too many things keep getting in his way for him to be successful to any noticeable degree in his endeavor: giants have a dismaying tendency to become windmills, and proud castles suddenly collapse to the level of smelly inns. But at long last a moment comes when all circumstances seem to favor the fulfillment of his dream. I refer to the episode of his penance in Sierra Morena, the central episode, in all respects, of Part I. In the middle of the wilderness, far from the worlds of others, in intimate communion with nature, our protagonist finds the ideal stage for lifting his life to the level of art.

The solitude of Sierra Morena, and also some subtler reasons which I will mention later, lead our knight to the decision of imitating Amadís of Gaul, his favorite chivalresque hero. At one point in his life's story, Amadís had felt jilted by his beloved Oriana and had retired to the Peña Pobre to do penance. This is precisely what Don Quixote undertakes to do, not only as a behavioral emulation but also as an *artistic* imitation. As he tells his squire, "I would have you know that it is not only my wish to find the madman [that is to say, Cardenio, the other madman who has sought refuge in the Sierra Morena, and whom I will have to mention again] that draws me to these parts, but my intention of performing a deed here which will gain me perpetual renown and glory throughout the known world. It shall be such a deed that by it I shall attain the utmost perfection and renown of which a knight-errant is capable."

Concerning his efforts to bring his life to "utmost perfection"—that is to say, to make it into a work of art—Don Quixote explains at length to his squire the Renaissance principle of the imitation of models. In his speech he continually mixes aesthetics and life, as becomes clear from his opening remarks, which could be taken from Giorgio Vasari or from just about any other sixteenth-century theoretician of art. As our protagonist says, warming up to his subject, "when any painter wishes to win fame in his art, he endeavours to copy the pictures of the most excellent painters he knows. . . ." And he concludes with the following syllogistic corollary: "I conclude that the knight errant who best copies him [Amadís] will attain most nearly to the perfection of chivalry." It should be clear now that Don Quixote confuses, no doubt on purpose, artistic imitation (legitimate in painting, as he reminds us) and the emulation of conduct. A normal knight-errant, if ever there were a normal one, might seek to emulate Amadís's conduct, his fortitude, sincerity, and devotion, but he would not seek to imitate the circumstances attending the various episodes of his life, in which his conduct was displayed. When the latter happens, we are confronted with someone who is trying to live life as a work of art.

What has prompted Don Quixote to come to this extraordinary decision in the middle of the Sierra Morena is, to hear him tell it, a forceful act of will. His action at this point is totally unmotivated, for, as he readily admits, he has no cause for complaint against Dulcinea del Toboso, as Amadís had against Oriana. Upon hearing of his master's decision to do penance, Sancho comments: "It seems to me . . . that the knights who did things like that were provoked and had a reason for their follies and penances. But what reason has your worship for going mad? What lady has scorned you, or what evidence have you found that the lady Dulcinea del Toboso has done anything she shouldn't with Moor or Christian?" To which his master replies: "That is the point . . . and in that lies the beauty of my plan. A knight errant who turns mad for a reason deserves neither merit nor thanks. The thing is to do it without cause; and then my lady can guess what I would do in the wet if I do all this in the dry."

I want to invite you at this point to forget for a while, if at all possible, the levity of tone of those speeches and to look at the moral implications of Don Quixote's action. Clearly it is totally lacking in motivation. It is only a sheer act of will that supports his life at this moment. Nothing in reality warrants either his action or the twist he has given to his life. Normally our will, guided by our conscience, desires one objective rather than another (fame instead of money, honesty instead of success, or vice versa), and we then support our will with the full strength of the combined reserves of our life. But at this point in our knight's career this normal relationship is presented exactly in reverse. It is his life now that has no other support but his will. Here we have something like the circus acrobat who stands himself on his index finger.

If you will allow me a brief truism, we normally conceive of the body as pushing the index finger, and not the other way around. The results of the latter could be calamitous. This is one way of saying that our whole life is predicated on the normal functioning of the eternal relations between subject and object. But with Don Quixote in Sierra Morena it looks more as if his will has become its own subject and object, much in the manner that the index finger of the circus acrobat is both his index finger and its own whole support.

The gravest of disruptions in the order of life has taken place at this point because, as the inescapable consequence of all the preceding, the normal relationship between cause and effect has ceased to exist. And the knowledge that a certain cause will bring about a certain effect is a prime factor in giving meaning, unity, and direction to our lives.

This most serious disruption in the eternal scheme of things is what the modern moralists call the gratuitous act. And with Don Quixote doing penance in Sierra Morena we are confronted with what may be the first gratuitous act in literature. This appears to be the first instance, in Western literature at least, in which a creative writer has set out to explore the problems that arise when a man's will becomes its own conscience.

A brief excursion into more modern literary history will show some of the implications of Don Quixote's action, which opened a Pandora's box of moral issues. Our modern age has given to moral issues the place that metaphysical issues used to have, and consequently the problem of individualism has been completely refocused. In my opinion, the greatest pioneer in the intellectual overhauling of individualism was Dostoevsky, who introduced the idea of a man-God to succeed the God-man. It is no coincidence that from the time of his first great novel Dostoevsky explored the depths of the gratuitous act, the possibilities and consequences of man acting in complete freedom. Raskolnikov's murder of the old moneylender in *Crime and Punishment* is a gratuitous act, or at least that is the way Raskolnikov wants it understood. And five years later Dostoevsky gave the issue a most extensive treatment in *The Possessed*, in the almost endless arguments of Kirillov about God and suicide.

André Gide, a great admirer of Dostoevsky, left us a good book on the Russian novelist. He also left us another kind of tribute to Dostoevsky's influence on him, and to the moral involvement of them both with the problem of the gratuitous act. In *Les Caves du Vatican*, Lafcadio, Gide's version of the "free man," pushes a man off a train, though he has never seen him and stands to gain nothing. A senseless crime, like Raskolnikov's, but again, as in Raskolnikov's case, rationalized by the criminal in terms of a gratuitous act.

More recently, Albert Camus has demonstrated his allegiance to Dostoevsky and also to his own type of existentialism by dealing extensively with the gratuitous act—which earlier he exemplified novelistically in Meursault's crime in *L'étranger*—in one of the essays of *Le mythe de Sisyphe*. But there is no need to carry this exploration any farther, for I have achieved what I set out to do—show the difference between Don Quixote's gratuitous act and some of its latter-day versions.

The most obvious shared characteristic of the modern versions is the disappearance of any ethical sense of life. Basically, in these versions, life has become but a dimension of man's will. That is why Raskolnikov and Lafcadio can make criminal amoralism into a new social standard.

All this is a far cry from the actions of Don Quixote, which involve no crime. In his case all that is involved is an error, and this because, driven by his imaginative desire to live life as a work of art, he has allowed his will to become self-sufficient. His conscience has been pushed into the background, and his will has implemented the cravings of his imagination. A common enough occurrence in the life of Don Quixote, indeed, but always, on other occasions, some corrective has been there in the form of windmills or innkeepers.

The episode of the Sierra Morena is distinguished from the others in that, first, the circumstances could not have been more propitious to living life as a work of art, and, second, there is no apparent corrective. The lack of a corrective would be most unusual in Cervantes' works, however, and the fact is that the corrective is included even here, carefully wrapped in irony, a trademark of Cervantes' style. The author's reprimand is couched in the following terms, at the point where Sancho asks his master to perform a few mad pranks so that he may report them to Dulcinea: Don Quixote, "hurriedly stripping off his breeches, . . . stood in his skin and his shirt. And then, without more ado, he took two leaps into the air, and twice turned head over heels, revealing such parts of his person as caused Sancho to turn Rocinante's head for fear he might see them a second time." The laughter that this picture provokes is the author's rebuke to a man who thinks that in his life he can imitate art, regardless of any other consequences, and that in undertaking such an imitation he can liberate his will from his conscience.

Don Quixote's action has consequences of a type unexpected by him or his reader. In this respect and in the general fact that no incidents in the book remain without a sequel of some sort, the novelistic world of *Don Quixote* is like the literary antecedent of Lavoisier's law of the conservation of matter: nothing is lost, everything changes. The rebuke to the protagonist has been unworthy of him, and, in the last analysis, unworthy also of Cervantes. Ridicule can be corrective, but hardly exemplary, and exemplarity is one of the aims of Cervantes' art, as he made quite clear in his *Exemplary Novels*. So the episode of the gratuitous act has an exemplary sequel.

Sancho starts out to go back from Sierra Morena to Dulcinea's village, to report on his master's mad pranks. On his way he meets the priest and the barber and tells them of his master's doings, whereupon they both decide to get Don Quixote out of

Sierra Morena, by deceit, of course, and take him to his village. For this endeavor they will eventually enlist the help of Dorotea, who will pose as Princess Micomicona. They all go back to the wilderness, where Don Quixote has stayed, and Sancho invents some whopping lies about the interview he is supposed to have had with Dulcinea—an interview which never takes place except in his imagination. In the course of this conversation, Don Quixote says that "it is a great honour for a lady to have many knights-errant serving her, with no greater ambition than of serving her for what she is, and without hope of any other reward for their zeal than that she shall be pleased to accept them as her knights." And Sancho replies, "That's the kind of love . . . I've heard them preach about. They say we ought to love our Lord for Himself alone, without being moved to it by hope of glory or fear of punishment. Though as for me, I'm inclined to love and serve Him for"—and the translation here is my own—"what I could do for Him."[2]

Truth, once again, has spoken through the mouth of fools. What Sancho has just expressed is the only true and desirable gratuitous act. In the history of Spanish spirituality the kind of divine love which Sancho has tried to describe is called the mystical doctrine of pure love. Its most ardent expounder was Saint Juan de Avila, whose writings were St. Teresa's models. But its most concrete and perfect literary expression is to be found in an anonymous sonnet, approximately contemporary with our novel and entitled "A Cristo crucificado." Since I have not found an English translation worthy of it, and I certainly dare not attempt one, I quote the beginning of it in the original Spanish:

> No me mueve, mi Dios, para quererte,
> el cielo que me tienes prometido;
> ni me mueve el infierno tan temido
> para dejar por eso de ofenderte.

And it ends:

> . . . aunque cuanto espero no esperara,
> lo mismo que te quiero te quisiera.

This is the only proper and true form of the gratuitous act, not the one performed by Don Quixote. This is the one true liberation of the eternal relationship between cause and effect. Contrary to Don Quixote or Raskolnikov or Lafcadio, where a man's will becomes its own conscience—as here in Sancho's words and in the sonnet—we have the perfect illustration of how a man's conscience can become its own will. If this is Don Quixote's final rebuke, it should also be the reader's most profound edification.

This part of the analysis of the concept of life as a work of art has taken us quite far from our initial subject matter. Let us go back to the beginning of the episode of Sierra Morena, where that concept is best embodied, and look at it from another point of view. Wilhelm Dilthey, the great German philosopher and historian of ideas, once said that "life is, precisely, many-sidedness." Three centuries before him, Cervantes had built his entire poetic universe on exactly that same belief. Multiplicity of perspectives is, therefore, what any approach to Cervantes demands of the critic.

If you recall, I mentioned that Don Quixote is not the only lunatic loose in the Sierra Morena. Cardenio is also there. The knight and squire at first catch only a glimpse of him in the distance, jumping, half-naked, from rock to rock. Later they learn some of his story from a goatherd, who explains that Cardenio's ragged appearance is due to the fact that "he had . . . to fulfill a certain penance which had been laid on him for his many sins." Even later, Cardenio himself will start to tell them his own story only with the condition that he not be interrupted under any circumstances. Unfortunately he mentions *en passant* the name of Amadís. This triggers the imagination of Don Quixote, who interrupts him, and, to cut a long story short, everything ends in a frightful melee, in which Cardenio beats up knight, squire, and goatherd to his entire satisfaction.

In this brief outline I have left in, on purpose, the two elements that define Don Quixote's unheard of decision to do penance in imitation of Amadís. The idea of penance is, from the beginning, associated with Cardenio, and he himself introduces the name of Amadís. Both terms are associated in Don Quixote's subconscious, and thus the idea of imitating Amadís' penance takes form. What in the Knight's consciousness is a gratuitous act, modern psychoanalysis can explain as a subconscious and free association of ideas.

A more obvious relationship between Don Quixote and Cardenio occurs when the latter appears on the scene and the author describes him as "the Ragged Knight of the Sorry Countenance," as Don Quixote is "the Knight of the Sad Countenance." Clearly Cervantes wants his readers to accept Cardenio as some sort of *alter ego* for our knight. Accordingly, the episode of Sierra Morena begins as a pendular movement between madness (Don Quixote, Cardenio) and sanity (Sancho, the goatherd). We have the abnormal pole of the madmen, which by definition will be irrational and absurd, and the normal pole of Sancho and the goatherd, reasonable and sensible.

But this initial impression should quickly disappear as we read on. I have just mentioned the beating that Cardenio gives the other three characters. As he struts away victoriously, his victims moan and groan, but then, suddenly, "Sancho got up and, furious at his undeserved beating, ran to take vengeance on the goatherd," and a second and no less bloody melee takes place. I ask you, where is the logic of all this? Obviously, the seemingly normal world of Sancho and the goatherd is also governed by the irrational and the absurd.

This note sets the tone of the whole episode of Don Quixote's penance in Sierra Morena, which takes place shortly thereafter. Then, through the trickery of the priest, the barber, and Dorotea, which I have already mentioned, Don Quixote is coaxed out of the Sierra Morena, and the Sierra Morena interlude comes to an end. But just before they leave the Sierra, they run into Andrés, the young boy who, in one of the initial chapters, was seen tied to a tree and being beaten by his master until Don Quixote came to his rescue. But you will also recall that no sooner had the knight turned his back than the master tied Andrés to the tree and resumed the beating where he had left off. Now, in the Sierra, Don Quixote wants Andrés to tell his friends of his great deed of justice. Andrés certainly does tell of his beating, but adds, "your worship's to blame for it all." I ask you again: what logic is there in Andrés accusing Don Quixote of his beating? Is not Andrés' world also governed by the irrational and the absurd? Most significant of all is the fact that Don Quixote's penance is neatly framed by the irrational beating Sancho gave the goatherd, at the beginning, and the illogical accusation by Andrés of Don Quixote, at the end. Obviously our knight's gratuitous act, which is absurd because it is unmotivated, corresponds strictly to the absurdity of the reactions of Sancho and Andrés. If Don Quixote's world is governed by the logic of the absurd, the world of Sancho and Andrés can only be said to be governed by the absurdity of logic.

Where does this leave us with regard to the concept of life as a work of art? I am afraid that the episode of Sierra Morena does not provide the full answer, even if it does provide its best illustration. But I think I can safely advance the following preliminary conclusion: Cervantes sees nothing wrong in the concept of life as a work of art *in* itself, but obviously he sees quite a few serious things wrong with that concept *by* itself.

If we want to pursue the idea, the practice and the implications of life as a work of art, we must turn to the second part of the novel. There, in the central episode of the Cave of Montesinos, I think we find our answer. There is a most significant correspondence between the episode of the Cave and the episode of Sierra Morena. These are the only two instances in the book in which Don Quixote is left strictly alone (I do not count his first sally because this antedates the creation of Sancho), and in both instances the knight dreams about the perfect world of art, in the Sierra with his eyes open and in active imitation of it, in the cave with his eyes closed and in passive imitation of it.

Everything Don Quixote sees in the cave he sees in an actual dream. He sees some knights and ladies who are really characters out of some of the epic Carolingian ballads, namely Montesinos, Durandarte, and Belerma, who are dedicated to reliving their poetic legend, and he also sees his beloved Dulcinea. Now, in order to understand some very strange aspects of his dream, I must make it clear that Don Quixote has arrived at the cave with his will well-nigh broken. This most alarming situation is caused directly by a long series of deceits practiced on the knight by others, not by himself, deceits which offer him a false reality to contend with, falsified by others, not by himself. The series opens with the deceit of the priest and others to get the knight out of the Sierra, an episode which is central to the first part, even in a numerical way. And the most recent deceit in the series has been Sancho's bit of roguery in enchanting Dulcinea.

The trappings of Don Quixote's dream are not consonant at all with the poetic nature of its characters and its setting. Everything has a shoddy quality about it. Everything is run-down or moth-eaten, and the description of Belerma, a traditional beauty in the ballads, well exemplifies this: "She was beetle-browed and somewhat flat-nosed, with a large mouth and red lips. Her teeth, which she sometimes bared, appeared to be few and not very well placed." Dulcinea herself is but that same coarse, ugly, garlic-smelling peasant woman that Sancho made her out to be.

Small wonder that when our hero is pulled out of the cave and awakened he exclaims, "Now, indeed, I positively know that the pleasures of this life pass like a shadow and a dream, and wither like the flowers of the field." In the cave and in his dream Don Quixote has seen the real results of living life as a work of art, much in the same way that we, the readers, have seen some of them in the episode of the Sierra. But the knight's awareness of the inadequacy of his ideal of life must have antedated by quite some time the adventure of the cave. That is why his subconscious is so ready to attribute such absurd qualities to the characters of his dream. The one positive aspect of the dream sequence in the cave is that it reveals to readers the extent of Don Quixote's awareness of the total inadequacy of his ideal of life.

There are many more implications in the episode of the cave of Montesinos. However, I already have ferreted out of the episode those points which are essential to my present purposes. For example, the possibilities of living life as a work of art are presented as numerous, and potentially as innumerable. Thus we have Don Quixote, Montesinos, Durandarte, etc., each striving in his own way to bring his life to the level of art. But the possibilities of achieving that end turn out to be a mirage. Even creatures of art, such as Montesinos and his companions, become worn-down and debased when they try to relive even their own poetry. If this is the case with creatures who were actually born within the realm of art, a mere mortal such as Don Quixote should expect only defeat and ridicule.

Furthermore, there are inherent dangers in trying to live art, as the analysis of the Sierra Morena episode should make clear. The dangers are those of considering that a thing which is good *in* itself, should be even better *by* itself, which is tantamount to turning a relative value into an absolute one. Fundamentally, however, the chief danger lies in the fact that art is man-made, whereas man (thank God!) is not. Therefore, trying to live life as a work of art represents a hopeless confusion of aims.

To this point and to this extent the protagonist of the novel is sharply reprimanded at almost every turn, and punished accordingly. But if we turn back for the last time to the episode of the cave of Montesinos, we shall see that once the knight has been dragged out of the cave and has been awakened, and after he pronounces those words which I quoted a short time ago, he dons his suit of armor again, and again sets himself to living life as a work of art, even though beset by ever-growing doubts. And this will go on to his dying day, when on his death-bed he abdicates his artistic personality by a last and supreme act of will. "Congratulate me, good sirs," he says, "for I am Don Quixote de la Mancha no longer, but Alonso Quixano, called for my way of life the Good." With his last actions the protagonist has performed the supreme sacrifice, the sacrifice of the self. Don Quixote, the creature of art, is to die, if Alonso Quixano, the creature of God, is to live.

But virtually until the protagonist enters eternity he has tried as valiantly as he could to live life as a work of art, in spite of rebukes and ridicule, and, by the time of the adventure of the cave of Montesinos, in spite of his knowledge of the inadequacy of his ideal. The episode of the Sierra Morena teaches the dangers of the ideal; the episode of the cave shows its vanity. But it is the words of Don Quixote coming out of the cave which contain the most valid and most human message of all, particularly to a world as sick as ours. Don Quixote has found out that trying to live life as a work of art is all vanity, for life is but a shadow and a dream. Yet he will go back to his ideal, even if he himself is eaten away by doubts, and he will pretend, heroically, that life is not just a shadow and a dream. In so doing, paradoxically, he prepares himself for an exemplary Christian death. And so should we.

Notes

1. All quotations from *Don Quixote* are taken from the Penguin translation by J. M. Cohen (Baltimore, 1964; first pub. 1950). Annotating a lecture on *Don Quixote*, however, is either a labor worthy of Hercules or a very perfunctory affair. My dear friend E. C. Riley (University of Edinburgh) and I have combined our efforts to give the best bibliography on the subject in our *Suma Cervantina* (London, 1973). If the reader is interested in pursuing any of the subjects hinted at in the present essay, I should like to refer him to that collaborative volume.

2. Since my interpretation of this passage rests heavily on the last words here, and since all the English translations I have consulted (with no intention of being exhaustive, I should add) deface to some extent Cervantes' thought at this point, I think it only proper to cite his own words: "Con esa manera de amor—dijo Sancho—he oído yo predicar que se ha de amar a Nuestro Señor, por sí solo, sin que nos mueva esperanza de gloria o temor de pena. Aunque yo le querría amar y servir por lo que pudiese." That the subject of *pudiese* is *yo* (not *él*, as commonly understood by translators) is made clear by Don Quixote's answer to Sancho: "¡Válate el diablo por villano—dijo Don Quixote—y qué de discreciones dices a las veces! No parece sino que has estudiado." Don Quixote would not be astonished at all if he understood Sancho to be thinking of what God could do for him (the normal point of our prayers) rather than of that sublimely naive vice versa, what *he* could do for God.

Appendix

Seminars of the Sixth Session of the Southeastern Institute
of Medieval and Renaissance Studies
15 July–23 August 1974

I. THE MEDIEVAL HOUSEHOLD

Senior Fellow: Dr. David Herlihy, Professor of History, Harvard University. Professor of History, University of Wisconsin (1964–70; William F. Allen Professor, 1970–72), Directeur d'études associé, Ecole Pratique des Hautes Etudes, VI Section, Paris (1969–70), Professor, Harvard (1972–). Fulbright Fellow (1954–55), Guggenheim Fellow (1961–62), ACLS Fellow (1966–67), President, Midwest Medieval Conference (1970–71), Fellow Mediaeval Academy of America (1971), Fellow at Center for Advanced Study in the Behavorial Sciences, Stanford (1972–73). Editor: *Medieval Culture and Society* (1968), *Economy, Society and Government in Medieval Italy*, with Robert S. Lopez and Vsevolod Slessarev (1969), *The History of Feudalism* (1970). Author, *Pisa in the Early Renaissance* (1958), *Medieval and Renaissance Pistoia* (1967), "Quantification and the Middle Ages," in *The Dimensions of the Past: Materials, Problems, and Opportunities for Quantitative Work in History*, ed. Val R. Lorwin and Jacob M. Price (1972), "Three Patterns of Social Mobility in Medieval History," *Journal of Interdisciplinary History*, 3 (1973), 623–647, etc.

Description: The evolution of the medieval household and family from the Carolingian epoch through the fifteenth century. The seminar reviewed the basic sources illuminating the family in medieval history, and it examined the forces which affected family life between the ninth and fifteenth centuries.

Fellows

Jane K. Beitscher (History, Univ. of California at Riverside)
Leroy J. Dresbeck (History, Western Washington State College)

Appendix

Theodore Evergates (History, Western Maryland College)
Francis X. Hartigan (History, Univ. of Nevada at Reno)
Winifred J. Mulligan* (History, North Carolina State Univ.)
Karina Niemeyer* (Romance Languages, Univ. of Michigan)
Theodore J. Rivers (History, no current affiliation)
Jon N. Sutherland (History, California State Univ. at San Diego)
Barbara H. Westman (Medieval and Renaissance Studies, UCLA)
* Auditing Fellow

II. MEDIEVAL VIRTUES AND VICES

Senior Fellow: Dr. Siegfried Wenzel, Professor of English and of
Comparative Literature, University of North Carolina, Chapel Hill.
Since September, 1974, Professor of English, University of Pennsylvania. ACLS Fellow (1964–65), Guggenheim Fellow (1968–69). Author, *The Sin of Sloth: Acedia in Medieval Thought and Literature*
(1967), "The Three Enemies of Man," *Mediaeval Studies*, 29 (1967),
47–66, "The Seven Deadly Sins—Some Problems of Research," *Speculum*, 40 (1968), 1–22, "Robert Grosseteste's Treatise on Confession,
'Deus est,' " *Franciscan Studies*, 30 (1970), 218–293, "The Source for
the *Remedia* of the Parson's Tale," *Traditio*, 27 (1971), 433–453, etc.

Description: Studies in the history and influence of the traditional
vices and virtues as they were "fixed" in such medieval schemes as
the Seven Deadly Sins, the theological-and-cardinal virtues, or the
remedial virtues. The seminar examined the appearance of the vices
and virtues in relevant pastoral literature, i.e., treatises on penance
and confession, sermons, handbooks for preachers, and related works
written in Latin and the vernacular languages between 1220 and
1450; and it explored their representation and iconography as well
as their use for purposes of structure, characterization, moral allegory, etc., in works of imaginative literature.

Fellows

Roger J. Adams (Art, SUNY at Brockport)
Joan H. Blythe (English, Univ. of Kentucky)
D. Peter Consacro (English, Univ. of Tennessee)
Eugene J. Crook (English, Florida State Univ.)
Ralph Hanna III (English, Univ. of California at Riverside)

Appendix

Kenneth J. Pennington (History, Syracuse Univ.)
Stephen L. Wailes (German, Indiana Univ.)

III. ATTRIBUTES SACRED AND SECULAR

Senior Fellow: Dr. William S. Heckscher, Benjamin N. Duke Professor of Art, Duke University. Associate Professor and Professor at the State University of Iowa (1947–55), Professor and Director of the Institute of Iconology, University of Utrecht (1955–66), Andrew Mellon Professor, Pittsburgh (1963–64), Director of Duke University Art Museum (1966–73), Professor, Duke (1966–74). Institute for Advanced Study, Princeton (1936–40, 1947–48, 1951–53, 1960–61) editor-in-chief of the *Netherlands Yearbook for Art History* (1959, 1960). Author, *Die Romruinen* (1936), *What Pictures Are Made Of* (Art Treasures of the World, 1953), *Art and Literature* (Art Treasures of the World, 1954), *Sixtus IIII Aeneas Insignes Statuas Romano Populo Restituendas Censuit* (Inaugural Address, Utrecht, 1955), *Rembrandt's "Anatomy of Dr. Nicolaas Tulp"* (1956), "Emblem, Emblembuch" (with Karl-August Wirth), *Reallexikon zur Deutschen Kunstgeschichte*, V, cols. 85–228 (1959), "The Annunciation of the Mérode Altarpiece. An Iconographic Study," in *Miscellanea Jozef Duverger* (1968), *Maces. An Exhibition of American Ceremonial Academic Scepters* (1970), etc.

Description: The role, form, and function of attributes of saints, princes of the Church and Realm, and commoners in the late Middle Ages and Renaissance. Often it is possible to identify a person in a portrait, allegory, or *portrait moralisé* if one has some knowledge of attributes such as emblems of martyrdom, attributive hints at legendary traits, insignia and badges, haloes, and musical and other instruments. This seminar was designed to serve the interests of art historians and literary historians.

Fellows

Charles M. Borkowski (German, UNC at Chapel Hill)
Gloria K. Fiero (History, Univ. of Southwestern Louisiana)
John S. Groseclose (German, Univ. of Illinois at Chicago Circle)
Paul F. Reichardt (English, Drury College)

Appendix

Gerald J. Schiffhorst (English, Florida Technological Univ.)
Steven N. Zwicker (English, Washington Univ.)

IV. THE REFORMATION AND SOCIAL CHANGE

Senior Fellow: Dr. Hans J. Hillerbrand, Professor of History and Dean of Graduate Studies, Graduate School and University Center of the City University of New York. Professor, Duke University (1967–70), Visiting Professor, University of Munich (1969), Professor, CUNY (1970–). *Journal of Medieval and Renaissance Studies*, Editorial Board (1965–), American Society for Reformation Research, Council (1966–69), Secretary (1969), Vice President (1971–72), President (1973–), American Society for Church History, Council (1971–). Editor, *A Bibliography of Anabaptism 1520–1630* (1962), *The Reformation: A Narrative History as Related by Contemporary Observers* (1965), *The Protestant Reformation: Select Documents* (1967), *Erasmus and His Age: Selected Letters* (1971). Author, *A Fellowship of Discontent* (1967), *Landgrave Philipp of Hesse, 1504–1567: Religion and Politics in the Reformation* (1967), *Men and Ideas in the 16th Century* (1969), *Christendom Divided: The Protestant Reformation* (1971), etc.

Description: The seminar addressed itself to an examination of the interaction between the Reformation (as a religious and theological movement) and society, particularly those facets of society undergoing dramatic changes in the first half of the sixteenth century. Among the topics discussed were education, women, and legislation for the poor. In each instance the focus was on the impact, both theoretical and practical, of the Reformation on society.

Fellows

Peter M. Ascoli (History, Utah State Univ.)
Frank Baron (German, Univ. of Kansas)
Phillip N. Bebb (History, Ohio Univ.)
Bodo Nischan (History, East Carolina Univ.)
James H. Overfield (History, Univ. of Vermont)
Ronald L. Pollitt (History, Univ. of Cincinnati)
Cyriac K. Pullapilly (History, St. Mary's College)

Appendix

Senior Fellow: Dr. Giles E. Dawson. Curator of Books and Manuscripts, Folger Shakespeare Library (1946–68), Professor of English, Catholic University of America (1967–71), Emeritus Professor and Senior Lecturer, Catholic University (1971–73), Assistant Professor, Howard University (1973–). Editor, *The Seven Champions of Christendome* (1929), *Joseph Quincy Adams Memorial Studies*, with James G. McManaway and Edwin E. Willoughby (1948), *Records of Plays and Players in Kent, 1450–1642* (1965), etc. Author, *The Life of William Shakespeare*, Folger Booklet No. 4 (1958), *Four Centuries of Shakespeare Publication*, University of Kansas Publications, Library Series 22 (1964), *Elizabethan Handwriting 1500–1650*, with Laetitia Kennedy-Skipton (1966), etc.

Description: The chief aim of the seminar was to develop in its members some facility in reading the "secretary" hand—the ordinary hand for business, correspondence, and literary composition in the sixteenth century. This involved a familiarity with the letter forms and mechanics of writing the hand, with common abbreviations and contractions, and with common spelling variants. According to the wishes of a majority of Fellows in the seminar, medieval text hands and court hands were also considered briefly.

Fellows

Richard C. Barnett (History, Wake Forest Univ.)
Thomas L. Berger (English, St. Lawrence Univ.)
Joyce H. Brodowski (Library, Trenton State College)
Samuel G. Hornsby, Jr. (English, LaGrange College)
Clarence H. Miller (English, St. Louis Univ.)
Michael Rudick (English, Univ. of Utah)
Jerry W. Williamson (English, Appalachian State Univ.)
Kenneth J. Wilson (English, Univ. of Rochester)

Senior Fellow: Dr. Juan Bautista Avalle-Arce, William Rand Kenan, Jr., Professor of Spanish, University of North Carolina, Chapel Hill. Professor of Spanish, Smith College (1961–65; Sophia Smith

Professor of Hispanic Studies, 1965–69). Premio Literario del Centro Gallego (1948), Guggenheim Fellow (1960–61), Bonsoms Medal (Government of Spain, 1962), ACLS Grant (1962, 1967–68), NEH Fellow (1967–68), National Board of Advisors, Instituto Cultural Hispánico (Spain, 1966–), editorial Board of *Anales Galdosianos* (1966–) and *Romance Monographs* (1968–), editor of *Studies in the Romance Languages and Literatures (UNCSRLL)*. Editor, *La Galatea*, Cervantes (1961, 1968), *Sumario de la natural historia de las Indias*, Gonzalo Fernández de Oviedo (1962), *Cervantes: Three Exemplary Novels* (1964), *Los trabajos de Persiles y Sigismunda*, Cervantes (1969), *Ocho Entremeses*, Cervantes (1970), *Morsamor*, Juan Valera (1970). Author, *Conocimiento y vida en Cervantes* (1959), *La novela pastoril española* (1959), *Deslindes cervantinos* (1961), etc.

Description: The main concern of the seminar was Cervantes' literary achievements, his novelistic, ideological, and thematic development. The approach was critical rather than linguistic, textual, or biographical, although topics touched upon his language and versification (lyric and dramatic). Participants were free to concentrate on any of Cervantes' works or any appropriate critical problem.

Fellows

John J. Allen (Romance Languages, Univ. of Florida at Gainesville)
A. F. Michael Atlee (Foreign Languages, California State Univ. at Los Angeles)
Mac E. Barrick (Foreign Languages, Shippensburg State College)
Constance A. Jordan (Comparative Literature, Yale Univ.)
Howard Mancing (Romance Languages, Univ. of Missouri)
Peter C. Marlay (Romance Languages, Case Western Reserve Univ.)